Intentional Community

Intentional Community

HOW *to* CHOOSE COMMUNITY LIVING
for BETTER HOUSING, HEALTH,
and HAPPINESS

Cynthia Tina

Copyright © 2025 by Cynthia Tina

All rights reserved. No part of this book may be reproduced, distributed, or transmitted in any form or by any means, including photocopying, recording, or other electronic or mechanical methods, without the prior written permission of the publisher, except in the case of brief quotations embodied in critical reviews and certain other noncommercial uses permitted by copyright law.

For permission requests, contact:
Community Finders
www.communityfinders.com

ISBN: 979-8-9943058-0-5

Printed in the United States of America

This book provides information and resources based on the author's experience visiting and working with intentional communities. It is not a substitute for legal, financial, or professional advice. Readers should consult appropriate professionals before making major decisions related to housing, finance, or relocation.

Edited by Chris Roth, editor of *Communities* magazine since 2008.

DEDICATION

To my parents, for their trust and support,
even when I did not make it easy.

TABLE OF CONTENTS

My Community Journey — 1
Your Community Journey — 9

Part I:
The Call to Community

Why Community — 21
What Is an Intentional Community? — 31
Types of Intentional Communities — 41

Part II:
Discovering Your Path

Envisioning Your Community Future — 65
Creating Your Community Wishlist — 73
Types of People Drawn to Community — 77
Are You Ready for Community Living? — 87
Creating Your Community Resume — 97

Part III:
The Search for Community

Researching Communities	105
Contacting Communities	113
Visiting Communities	121
Vetting Communities	135
Stepping Into Membership	141

Part IV:
Practical Considerations

How Much Does It Cost?	153
Finding a Diverse Community	167
Finding Community as an Elder	177
Raising Children in Community	185
Joining a Community Abroad	193

Part V:
Starting a Community

Should You Start a Community?	205
Advice for Starting a Community	213

Part VI:
Preparing for Community

How Do Communities Work?	235
When Conflict Happens	243

Part VII:
Closing Thoughts

A Winter Day in Community	255
Defending Your Choice	259
The Future of Community	267
Where to Go Next	279
Author Notes and Acknowledgments	281
About the Author	285

MY COMMUNITY JOURNEY

> "Two roads diverged in a wood, and I—
> I took the one less traveled by,
> And that has made all the difference."
> —Robert Frost

As a teenager, I loved reading books like the one you're holding now.

Every trip to the bookstore, I'd head straight for a small back corner of the upstairs floor to the one section that held all my favorites. How-to manuals on natural building and organic gardening, guides to wild food foraging, environmental exposés, and stories about people who had created lives outside the ordinary.

This book didn't exist then, but if it had, I would have devoured it.

Those books planted a seed in me. My love for reading about alternative living soon became a longing to experience it myself.

The First Step

When I was fifteen, I read *The Last American Man*, the story of Eustace Conway, a student of Native American lifeways and survival skills. When I learned he had started a center, called Turtle Island Preserve in North Carolina, I had to go. I asked my mom if I could spend a summer there for an immersion program, and she said yes (thank you mom!).

So off I went, flying alone from Massachusetts to Boone, North Carolina. It was my first real adventure into another way of living. We slept in simple cabins, cooked over open fires, milked goats, wove flax into linen, held traditional sweat lodges, and practiced night vision in the woods. I remember the feeling of belonging to something bigger than myself. In many respects, it was probably my first "intentional community" experience.

On the long drive back to the airport, I shared with the program leader about my trepidations of returning to "normal life." I knew my family and friends at school wouldn't be able to relate to the experiences I had that summer. I questioned my ability to stay true to my own calling, while surviving two more years of private Catholic high school.

She turned to me and said, "Sounds like you're walking the line."

"What does that mean?" I asked.

"It means you're walking the line between worlds. There's a thin line between mainstream culture and this way of living we have here. You can help people see that there's something else possible."

That conversation so long ago has profoundly shaped what my life's work has become—a bridging between worlds.

Walking Between Worlds

I grew up in the suburbs outside Boston. Catholic school uniforms, family dinners, and summer camp were all part of the routine. My parents both worked conventional jobs, and my younger sister has followed a similar path. By most accounts, I was supposed to do the same.

But even as a kid, I felt something different stirring in me. I spent hours exploring the woods behind our house, tending a small vegetable garden in the backyard, making herbal medicines, and proudly bringing my homegrown purple carrots to school lunches. My friends didn't quite get it, but I loved the feeling of creating something real and alive.

That curiosity eventually led me further afield.

After high school graduation, I asked my mom if I could volunteer for the summer in Kenya, East Africa. Again, she said yes! There I learned about permaculture and biodynamic farming, testing my fortitude with local villagers who could not understand why this privileged white girl would travel all this way to talk to them about going back to farming the way *their grandparents did*. They wanted to use pesticides and all the modern technology that had gotten us Westerners ahead.

I was beginning to grapple with questions bigger than I knew how to answer.

My college admissions essay was about my experiments gathering wild acorns and processing them into flour each autumn. That got me into St. Lawrence University, right near the border of Canada, home of Amish and back-to-the-land farmers who taught me so much about simple living. There I helped start a campus garden and had my first forays into community organizing. After a semester program on a remote lakeshore in the Adirondacks living in a small village of yurts with eleven other students, the idea of returning to normal classrooms for my sophomore year was unthinkable. I wanted out. My parents weren't so keen on a college dropout for a daughter, so I found a middle way through the low-residency school of Goddard College. There I was able to earn a degree in Sustainability, while traveling to study intentional communities in Africa, India, Central America, and Europe.

I lived for stretches at Sirius Ecovillage in Massachusetts, in urban co-ops in Asheville, in a charming hilltop community in the Mediterranean, and even helped start a new ecovillage in Togo, West Africa. That project ultimately didn't succeed, but it taught me more about community and cross-cultural collaboration than any classroom ever could.

I also dove deep into the networks that support these projects around the world. My entry point came during a stretch of solo travel through Europe. The final stop on my itinerary was a gathering that kept showing up in my research, so I took it as a sign I had to go. It was the annual Global Ecovillage Network (GEN) Conference, held at a different European community each year.

After winding through the valleys of the Swiss Alps, the bus carried me higher and higher until I reached Schwibenalp, the Center of Unity and host for the 2013 GEN Conference. The mountains were almost unreal in their beauty. I stepped off the bus into a swirl of bright skirts, strangers hugging, and conversations in half a dozen languages.

Initially, it all was too much. I felt like I had stumbled into the heart of hippie land, and even I (with all my alternative life choices) was altogether too conventional to fit in.

Then something in me softened. I could feel the pull of belonging, and with it the sense that I might have a role to play here. My privilege had enabled me to travel the world and learn from diverse communities. Now I wanted to use it in a way that mattered. I wanted to contribute to the movement that was welcoming me in.

That week opened a door for me. I joined the youth branch of the Ecovillage Network, which gave me a sense of purpose when I returned to the United

States. I kept going back to GEN gatherings year after year, eventually serving on the board and taking on coordinator roles. Later, I became involved with the Foundation for Intentional Community (FIC), where I helped lead a rebranding effort, served on the board, and later held a director role.

I am proud to still work with these organizations and many others that are uplifting a vast movement of intentional communities. The people within this movement have been my greatest teachers. Their work, ideas, and wisdom grace every page of this book.

Finding Home

After years of travel, I began to crave roots.

I had visited hundreds of communities. Grand and exotic ones like Auroville in India and Damanhur in Italy. Places at the forefront of movement building and experimentation.

But this country mouse wanted a quiet, peaceful community to call home. After falling in love with the seasons and landscapes of Vermont at an early age, I always thought I'd end up there. And so it has come to pass.

In 2019, I joined Headwaters Community, a small ecovillage tucked into the hills of northern Vermont. Eight households share fourteen acres here at the headwaters of the Winooski River. Our homes are close together, surrounded by gardens, bees, chickens, and forest paths.

When I first arrived, I promised my new neighbors I wouldn't be gone more than four months a year. After a decade of moving around, I was ready to build something lasting.

My home here is still a work in progress. I've built it slowly, with the help of my dad, neighbors, friends, and my own two hands. The house is a mix of natural and conventional techniques, with charred wood siding, clay-lime plaster walls, and a sun-filled greenhouse for passive solar heating.

My dear house is itself a bridge between worlds. It has taught me about compromise, hard work, the follies of idealism, and endless patience.

They say when you build your own house it's never done. So far, this has proven true. Once a year, I host a group of visitors who come see my house and community as part of the Vermont Ecovillage Tour. My initial anxiety about strangers seeing all the unfinished messiness has eased somewhat. I know the story of every inch of this place. My tears and love are (quite literally) plastered into the walls. What people see is a living story, still unfolding.

From this home of mine, I get to plug into a global network of intentional communities. When I'm not caked in dirt from an afternoon of gardening or plastering, I'm speaking and teaching about community living, nicely presentable on Zoom.

I run a travel company called Ecovillage Tours that helps people visit communities in person. We host trips that you can join across Europe, Asia, Central America, and North America. Explore upcoming trips at **ecovillagetours.com.**

I host online programs for people searching for community and write about the journey at Community Finders. Much of what you'll read here started as blog posts on **communityfinders.com.**

The other part of my time is spent being a member of Headwaters. Community life isn't perfect. We've had disagreements, long meetings, and moments of frustration. But we've also built a wood-fired sauna, brought in the garlic harvest each autumn, shared countless meals, watched kids grow up, and gathered around fires that burn late into the night.

This is my home, and I love it.

Bringing Others Home

Finding my own home at Headwaters was only part of the story. The other part has been helping other people find theirs.

Over the years, I've sat down with more than four hundred individuals and families searching for a place where they can belong. My clients have come from every walk of life you can imagine. Retirees craving connection, young families looking for support, dreamers, healers, activists, people craving more for their one wild and precious life.

As a "community matchmaker," I began helping them sort through the landscape of intentional communities and identify places that might be a fit. Bit by bit, I built a privately curated directory. I became the person who knew which communities were thriving, which were just forming, which had challenges under the surface, and which would resonate with a particular personality or lifestyle. I've visited many myself or interviewed them on the Virtual Tour of Intentional Communities show.

This matchmaking work has shaped this book more than anything else. It has forced me to learn the joining process inside and out. Not just through my own story, but through the journeys of hundreds of people I've guided along the way.

Over the past decade, my life has revolved around helping people find, join, and start intentional communities. Through Community Finders and Ecovillage Tours, I've had the privilege of introducing thousands of people to places and relationships that have changed their lives.

At the same time, the world around us is changing. Remote work has opened new possibilities. The housing crisis has pushed many to rethink affordability and ownership. Loneliness has become a public health issue. And in response, a modern wave of intentional communities—ecovillages, cohousing neighborhoods, homesteading collectives, and cooperative living models—has been steadily rising.

I wrote *Intentional Community: How to Choose Community Living for Better Housing, Health, and Happiness* as an entry point for this moment. A grounded guide with practical steps on how to find a community to join, start one yourself, or simply create more connection wherever you live now.

This is not a utopian vision. It's a practical guide from someone who has lived it, witnessed it, and walked alongside hundreds of people seeking the same thing: a place to belong.

YOUR COMMUNITY JOURNEY

> "It is no measure of health to be well adjusted to a profoundly sick society."
>
> —Jiddu Krishnamurti

If you're dreaming about community life and wondering how to make it real, you're not alone.

All around the world, people are quietly opting out of the default script—work, commute, consume, scroll, sleep, repeat—and choosing to return to something older, softer, and more human: living in community.

You're not crazy for wanting that. You're not naïve. You're not even all that radical.

You're just following your evolutionary programming.

For nearly all of human history, living outside of community wasn't just unusual, it was dangerous. We relied on each other for food, safety, care, belonging, purpose, and identity. "My people" wasn't a slogan. It was survival.

Now we live in a time where it's possible, at least logistically, to get through a week with almost no meaningful human contact. You can work from home, order groceries, eat dinner alone, fall asleep in front of a glowing screen, and repeat. You can own every tool, every appliance, every subscription, and never have to knock on a neighbor's door. You can live next to someone for five years and never learn their name.

That level of independence is convenient. It is also making us deeply unwell.

Loneliness is now being called one of the biggest health crises of our time. Rates of anxiety, isolation, and burnout keep climbing. Many people are barely holding their lives together, and doing it alone. Meanwhile, the cost of housing has become unsustainable for millions, and fear about the future—climate, safety, stability—is an unnerving undertone to our daily lives.

So if some part of you is whispering, "There has to be another way," that part of you is wise.

This book is, quite literally, about that other way.

Why You're Here

If you've picked up this book, chances are you're ready for a change.

Maybe you're tired of doing everything alone—childcare, eldercare, emotional care, financial stress, meals, holidays, decisions, home maintenance, health scares, all of it.

Maybe you're craving a sense of belonging. Not just "friends I need to coordinate to meet up with" but "people who notice if I don't come home."

Maybe you've had a glimpse of what community could feel like: a nostalgic memory of college dorm living, kids running in a pack instead of isolated in bedrooms, neighbors stopping to chat on the front stoop, elders who are woven into daily life instead packed into nursing homes.

Or maybe you're on the other end. Maybe you're just done with the way things are. You don't want to pour your life's energy into paying for a home that keeps you isolated, consuming products to fill emotional gaps, and hoping the world will magically become more humane on its own. You want to be part of something that feels like a solution.

Wherever you are on that spectrum—exhausted, curious, hopeful, skeptical—this book is for you.

Because wanting community is one thing. Finding it, joining it, or creating it is another.

That's where most people get stuck.

Why This Isn't Just a "Feel Good" Book

This is not a book of utopian fantasies.

It's not "let's all buy land together and it will be perfect forever."

Anyone who has ever tried to live closely with other humans knows: community can be beautiful, and it can also be intense. Real people bring real needs, real trauma, real preferences about kitchen shelves and noise at 10 p.m. and who parks where.

Living in community is not for everyone. This way of life asks you to grow. It asks you to communicate clearly. It asks you to listen. It asks you to repair. It asks you to be honest about your needs and also honest about the fact that other people have needs too.

It is the most rewarding "hard work" many people ever do.

So this book is not here to sell you a fantasy.

It's here to help you build a life rooted in community.

Where You Are on the Journey

Most people who find their way to intentional community move through a similar arc. Over time I've come to think of it as a kind of Roadmap to Community. It rarely unfolds in a straight line, but the themes tend to rhyme.

1. The Awakening

For many people, the shift begins during a major life change. The pandemic was a big one for so many of us. Routines collapsed, remote work became possible, and suddenly people began asking where they actually wanted to live and who they wanted around them.

Parenthood can spark it too. You look at your child and think about the village you wish you had for them. The same can happen when the kids leave home, after a separation, or in the quiet of being widowed. Transition makes space for new questions.

Sometimes the spark is much smaller. International travel to a culture with more intact communities. A video of stunning natural building architecture that makes you wonder if you could ever live like that. Or a morning when you realize the neighbor you wave to every day is someone you've never really met.

Often, even before you learn the phrase "intentional community," something in you starts wondering if those old hippie communes still exist somewhere.

That moment, when possibility opens even a crack, is the beginning of the journey.

2. Deepening the Curiosity

Once the idea takes hold, the curiosity deepens. You want to understand how all of this works.

You find your way to some community websites, perhaps even whole online directories of ecovillages, tiny house communities, cohousing, and the like.

Then you learn about decision-making, conflict navigation, membership processes, and the communication skills that go along with intentional community living. You start to get clearer on what you want and what you don't. Maybe you begin to picture yourself living in a place like this.

Around this stage, people often reach out to me. More than one client has started our call in tears. I remember one woman telling me she felt embarrassed to admit how lonely she was, even though she lived in a "nice neighborhood" and had done everything she was told would lead to a good life. Naming her desire for community out loud felt like a release.

These moments of recognition are common, and they are meaningful. You begin to sense that community is not something that only other people do. It might be possible for you too.

3. Seeking

Eventually, reading and dreaming turn into action. You start visiting communities. You write to a few places, book a weekend stay, meet residents, walk the land. You pay attention to how you feel around the people, in the shared kitchen, during a meeting. You compare experiences. You narrow things down. You might join a waiting list or stay nearby for a few months. You begin to imagine how your actual life might fit there.

At the same time, an intentional community is getting to know you too.

This part can be exciting, tender, confusing, inspiring, and humbling all at once. Community becomes something you can touch. Something you can see yourself stepping into.

> "As you visit a community you enter a fertile, cross-pollination point—where the needs of the community and the community seeker come together—a time ripe with possibilities."
> —Diana Leafe Christian, *Finding Community*

4. Choosing the Path Ahead

From here, the road can go in a few different directions.

- A. **Some people find their place and join an existing community.** They apply, get accepted, and begin the slow process of integrating into a group that already has its rhythms and ways of doing things.
- B. **Others wait after finding a potential place.** They stay in touch, keep visiting, or realize this isn't their place after all.
- C. **Some decide they have to build something new.** This is the path of gathering people, shaping agreements, facing money and land decisions, navigating personalities, and holding a shared vision through many seasons of change. It's a big undertaking, but it can be deeply rewarding.
- D. **And some people stay where they are, not because the dream fades but because life asks them to remain rooted for now.** Kids in school. Work that can't be relocated. A partner who needs time. Health needs. Aging parents. When relocation isn't right, they may begin more intentionally weaving community into the life they already have. They host dinners, volunteer in the local garden, create childcare swaps, start a neighbor potluck, or turn a casual acquaintance into a real relationship. They build community in place.

Community is not only a destination. It's a way of moving through the world. Sometimes we go in circles—joining a community, leaving it, starting one, living alone awhile, coming back into a formal community or not.

Take a moment and locate yourself. Where are you on this path? Are you:

- Just discovering that intentional communities exist?
- Already visiting them?
- Quietly gathering a few friends who keep saying, "What if we…?"
- An elder who refuses to age alone?
- A parent thinking, "I can't raise kids like this anymore"?
- Someone who has never felt like they fit where they are?

Wherever you are, hold that. It will guide you as you move forward.

How to Use This Book

This book is designed to support your journey towards community with clear, practical steps and information. Here's a look at what's to come:

In Part I, *The Call to Community*, we'll explore why so many of us are feeling this pull right now and what "intentional community" actually means. There are dozens of models. By the end of this section, you'll have clearer language for what you're seeking instead of just a vague longing for "something different."

In Part II, *Discovering Your Path*, we'll turn inward. You'll reflect on your values, needs, and non-negotiables. You'll create your own Community Wishlist, the tool I use most often with clients. We'll also look at the fears and misconceptions that often derail people before they even start.

Part III, *The Search and the Visit*, gets practical. You'll learn how to find communities, how to reach out respectfully, what to pay attention to when you visit, and how to tell the difference between a healthy community and one that might be struggling.

Part IV, *Expanding Your Options*, is where we tackle real-life complexities. Money. Kids. Aging. Partners who aren't on board. International moves. The question of whether you want to join an existing community or start one.

Part V, *Living and Thriving in Community*, looks at what happens after you say yes. How communities actually function, how decisions get made, how conflict is handled, and how to prepare yourself so you don't arrive expecting a fantasy and leave when reality shows up.

By the end, you'll have a map and a set of next steps that you can actually take.

I've also created a companion collection of tools and resources at **communityfinders.com/book1**. There you'll find materials that would have made this book far too long to print, including worksheets you can edit directly and updated website links.

One More Thing Before We Begin

The biggest lie modern culture tells us is that you're supposed to do life alone. Some people genuinely enjoy living alone, and there is nothing wrong with that. But if you are feeling lonely more often than not, if a part of you aches for community, you need to know that there are options.

You don't have to keep doing everything in isolation—alone in your home, alone with your worries, alone with your aging body, alone with your grief, alone with your kids, alone with the fear that the world is changing faster than you can keep up.

It isn't working.

You're allowed to say that out loud.
You're allowed to want something better.
You're allowed to want people around you.
You're allowed to want a home that feels like belonging.

This book isn't here to convince you to want community. You already do. It's here to help you find your way back to it.

Let's begin.

PART I:

THE CALL TO COMMUNITY

WHY COMMUNITY

> "Because when there are too many strangers, strangerhood becomes a template for social engineering. The world is paying a heavy price for this. We can see it in how we feel: our radical loneliness, no matter who is around us, no matter how affluent and lucky we are."
>
> —Stephen Jenkinson

Why Community

When I lead workshops, I often begin with a simple question: Why community?

Why are you here? What is pulling you toward this idea of intentional community living?

People answer in different words, but the heart of it is usually the same. They want to live near others who share their values. They want support, and they want to be supportive. They want their lives to contribute to something that matters. They want to feel connected to a place and to the people in it. They want belonging.

Before you go much further in this book, take a moment and ask yourself the same thing.

Why community, for you?

You don't have to write an essay. Just name a reason. Now name another reason. Keep going until you feel you've gotten to the crux of it.

Say your reasons out loud or better yet, jot them down. Your reasons will guide you when it comes time to make real choices.

For some people the motivation is intimate and personal. They don't want to age alone. They want their children to grow up with other children, not just screens. They want people around them who will notice if something is wrong.

For others, the draw is more systemic. They no longer want to pour their one precious life into a culture that isolates and exhausts people, while depleting the planet. They want to be part of something that feels like a solution rather than another cog in the machine.

Both motivations belong here. Intentional community is not only a lifestyle. It is also a quiet kind of social activism. It is a way to live differently today instead of simply talking about what is broken.

The World We're Trying to Survive Right Now

Let's look for a moment at what is broken.

The crises of our times are overlapping and mounting. Loneliness. Housing. Climate. They are braided together, and most people feel the pressure in more than one place.

Let's start with loneliness, because it is not simply emotional pain. It is a public health crisis.

A 2023 advisory from the US Surgeon General, Dr. Vivek H. Murthy, is titled *Our Epidemic of Loneliness and Isolation*. The report begins:

"When I first took office as Surgeon General in 2014, I didn't view loneliness as a public health concern. But that was before I embarked on a cross-country listening tour, where I heard stories from my fellow Americans that surprised me.

"People began to tell me they felt isolated, invisible, and insignificant. Even when they couldn't put their finger on the word 'lonely,' time and time again, people of all ages and socioeconomic backgrounds, from every corner of the country, would tell me, 'I have to shoulder all of life's burdens by myself,' or 'if I disappear tomorrow, no one will even notice.'

"It was a lightbulb moment for me: social disconnection was far more common than I had realized.

"In the scientific literature, I found confirmation of what I was hearing. In recent years, about one-in-two adults in America reported experiencing loneliness. And that was before the COVID-19 pandemic cut off so many of us from friends, loved ones, and support systems, exacerbating loneliness and isolation."

Take that in for a moment longer: *half of all American adults experience loneliness.*

The Surgeon General goes on to link loneliness to greater risk of cardiovascular disease, dementia, stroke, depression, anxiety, and premature death. Loneliness has a mortality impact equivalent to smoking fifteen cigarettes a day. On the collective level, it fuels division that is tearing civil society apart. Dr. Murthy fears, "Instead of coming together to take on the great challenges before us, we will further retreat to our corners—angry, sick, and alone."

Life has changed dramatically in just a few decades. According to a Gallup poll in 1990, the average American had three close friends. By 2021, an American Perspectives Survey found that number had dropped to one, and twelve percent of people said they had none. Only sixteen percent of adults feel very attached to their local community. Seventy percent say they barely know their neighbors.

Meanwhile, digital life continues to expand. According to the *Digital 2024 Global Overview Report*, the typical internet user spends about **6 hours and 40 minutes online each day**. Americans and younger generations tend to spend even more. These devices are supposed to "connect us," yet many still feel starved for genuine connection.

Instead of facing the hassle and anxiety of meeting in person, it is often easier to retreat into our devices for the semblance of connection we find there. But with so many of us online, moments of real connection are precious few.

This is not a personal failure. It is structural. Humans evolved to live in villages and clans, surrounded by familiar faces, buffered by shared responsibility. The idea that a single household should carry the entire load is new, and it is breaking us.

Layer the housing crisis on top of that. Safe, stable housing is out of reach for many. Prices climb faster than wages. Renting is unstable. Homeownership is isolating and costly, with the median home price in the United States currently a staggering $400,000. The nuclear-family-in-a-house model all of our infrastructure is built around assumes you have a nuclear family, even as family sizes shrink and more people live alone than ever before.

And then there is the ecological crisis. Pollution, storms, fires, floods, supply chain disruptions. More and more people want to build resiliency through local food systems, renewable energy, and trusting relationships with neighbors who can be relied on in times of need. We urgently need to regenerate land and repair ecosystems through collective effort.

Loneliness. Housing challenges. Climate chaos. These are just three of the ills afflicting modern life, for which community could be an antidote. There are others I could name: systemic racism, widespread depression, rising surveillance and loss of privacy, political extremism. One of the most troubling for me is our growing inability to talk across differences.

Relatives who no longer speak because of elections, mandates, identity politics, moral lines in the sand. Conversations that once felt normal now feel dangerous.

The result is millions of people who are isolated, overloaded, financially stretched, frightened about the future, and unable to speak openly about any of it.

Community does not erase these pressures, but it offers a way to meet them *together*. The "together" piece is important here. Don't expect to agree with your community mates on every polarized issue. Instead of only seeking "like-minded" people, look for "like-hearted" people—those willing to engage across differences, build trust, and work toward shared solutions.

Community living solves many problems, but its real power is teaching us the skills we need to solve everything else.

What Community Can Actually Do

Let's talk about the solutions community living can offer in real terms.

Community reduces isolation. In a healthy intentional community, it is rare to go days without meaningful interaction. You see each other in the common house, pass each other on a path, share meals here and there. You are known.

Community creates a safety net. If you're sick, someone brings soup. If you're missing from a place you're usually seen, someone checks in. If you've had a rough day, you don't need to stick to "good" when asked how you are. There's the ability to be vulnerable and be held.

Community lightens the load. Instead of ten households buying and maintaining ten of everything, separately, many things are shared. Tools, rides, childcare, garden work, emotional support. Life can get cheaper, easier, and less frantic when it is not all on you.

Community builds resilience. Shared gardens, renewable energy systems, pooled funds, cooperative decision-making, conflict resolution skills, emergency plans. These are not theories. They exist in real communities right now.

Community allows you to live in alignment with your values. Many people want to live more sustainably and more cooperatively but have no idea how to do that in isolation. Community offers a structure that supports the life you want to live.

And perhaps the most underrated benefit: it makes life more joyful. Shared meals, spontaneous gatherings, kids playing together, late-night conversations, someone dropping off extra garden greens. Joy matters more than we acknowledge.

As Margaret Wheatley put it simply, "Whatever the problem, community is the answer."

Last winter was a fierce one here in Vermont. March buried us in snow and April sealed it in ice. One night, after a long freeze, I heard a deep creak followed by a heavy crash as a thick sheet slid from my roof. I didn't think much of it. Morning came, and I lit the woodstove as usual.

A few minutes later, there was a knock at the door. Far too early for a casual visit. My neighbor stood there. "Put out the stove," he said. "Your chimney is gone." The snow had sheared it clean off!

He didn't just notice. He acted. And that same evening, tools in hand, he had the whole thing repaired.

Where else could you live where someone would spot a danger like that, knock at dawn, and have both the skill and the willingness to fix it before nightfall?

"But Do I Lose My Independence?"

This is one of the biggest fears people carry in. They imagine a loss of privacy or autonomy. But intentional community is not about erasing individuality. It is about balancing independence *with interdependence.*

In almost every community I visit, people still have private homes or private rooms. They have doors that close. They have the freedom to opt in or out. What changes is that connection becomes available *if you choose.*

There's a common assumption that community people must be extroverts. In reality, many intentional communities are full of introverts. Why? Because introverts may find it hard to meet people in "normal life," so they seek out a living situation where social interaction is woven into daily life, *and* where the door can shut when alone time is needed.

This balance between autonomy and connection is something psychologist William Von Hippel explores in his book *The Social Paradox: Autonomy, Connection, and Why We Need Both to Find Happiness.* He argues that humans thrive when we feel both self-directed and supported, and that modern life has overcorrected toward independence at the cost of belonging.

Community living attempts to restore that balance in a very practical way.

The longest-running study on human happiness, the Harvard Study of Adult Development, reinforces this point. Beginning in 1938 and continuing for more than 85 years, it shows again and again that more than diet, income, or even genetics, the strongest predictor of a long and satisfying life is the quality of our close relationships. Meaningful social connection—feeling supported, seen, and woven into the lives of others—is one of the most powerful determinants of both health and happiness.

The dominant culture teaches that independence equals freedom. In reality, independence without any shared life often equals exhaustion. Community offers another kind of freedom, one where you are not carrying the full weight of living alone.

A few nights ago I heard a pitiful sound, some creature wailing into the night. I ran outside to realize it was my neighbor's pup, left home alone, stricken that his family was on an overnight trip away. Within a few minutes, more neighbors came out to comfort the pup who soon was back to tail-wagging glee.

I had to wonder. How many of us have lonely nights like that—where we wish we could just let out a howl and have caring people surround us?

This puppy gets to live within an intentional community. How very lucky he is.

The Emotional Shift

Living in community asks you to practice skills most of us were never taught in school: listening well, stating needs clearly, repairing after conflict, navigating differences, and being accountable to the people around you.

Most of us grew up in classrooms where everyone sat in rows with a teacher at the front. Community invites us to turn the chairs toward one another and become one another's teachers.

As Earthaven member Lee Warren once shared with me during an interview, "The most important things to know about being successful in community is to know how to self-regulate, to know our own window of tolerance, to grow our capacity for discomfort, to be able to be embodied, to not take things personally. When we become more emotionally intelligent, we can navigate the world through a sense of resiliency and give more than we need."

She emphasizes, "Community is the child, *not the parent*."

Being good parents. Raising up a community. Sitting in circle. This is not always easy. Some days it is humbling. Some days it is frustrating. Some days it is healing.

Community living is often described as a major personal growth workshop. It's like living in a hall of mirrors. The people around you reflect your strengths, your blind spots, your hopes, and your habits. Another metaphor I love is the rock tumbler—maybe you had one as a kid. A handful of rough stones go in, they tumble around together, bumping into one another, and if you stay with it long enough, they come out smoother, shinier, transformed. (Or at least we hope!)

Different intentional communities have different degrees of shared life. Some are highly collaborative, some are more private. Most ebb and flow over time with more or less interaction. Community isn't the right fit for everyone in every chapter of life.

The hardest part of community living? The people.

The best part of community living? The people!

Community stretches you in all the best ways. It gives you a way to practice being human—not perfectly, but honestly—alongside other people who are trying too.

And that practice, more than anything else, is what makes community worth it.

Why This Matters Even If You Never Join

You might be thinking that all of this sounds great but isn't realistic for your life right now. And that may be true. Most people cannot simply move to an ecovillage next month.

Even so, intentional communities matter.

As historian and anthropologist Kristen Ghodsee explains in her book *Everyday Utopia: What 2,000 Years of Experiments in Cooperative Living Teach Us About the Good Life*, the rise and fall of intentional communities throughout history is not proof that they don't work—it's proof that they matter.

Their continual reappearance across centuries and cultures shows that humans keep returning to this idea because it meets a deep and recurring need for connection, cooperation, and care that no other social model has fully satisfied.

Intentional communities are living laboratories where people are testing real-life solutions to the biggest questions we face.

How do we age with dignity?
How do we raise children without burning out?
How do we share resources sustainably?
How do we handle conflict without fracturing relationships?
How do we build resilience in a changing climate?
How do we create places where people actually thrive?

Communities are experimenting with these questions every day. You can borrow their tools and apply them in your own neighborhood or family circle. Your life does not have to be isolated to be independent.

This chapter has been about the "why." Why community matters. Why so many people are craving it at this particular moment. Why these longings are not personal quirks but responses to a world that no longer matches how humans are built to live.

In the next chapter, we will talk about what intentional communities actually are. How they're structured, what they look like day to day, what holds them together, and what you can expect if you move into one.

By the end, you will have real language for what you're seeking, not just the vague wish for "more community." You will know what kind of community fits you, and why.

WHAT IS AN INTENTIONAL COMMUNITY?

> "The more things fall apart—the more the centre cannot hold—the more new centres are seeded on the margins, which is the only place they can ever grow."
> —Paul Kingsnorth

In the last chapter we looked at *why* so many people are craving community right now. Loneliness, the cost of housing, climate stress, burnout from doing everything alone. Community can offer an antidote to many modern ailments.

Now let's talk about what that actually looks like in practice.

Because "community" can mean a lot of things.

I like to think that we all live in and among communities. Think of your family, a school, church, sports team, or even online community you may be part of. These communities have varying degrees of intentionality around the "community" part. Meanwhile, *intentional* communities are groups at the far end of the spectrum. They exist to foster community, their purpose (at least in part) is to build social connection and group cohesion.

For the purposes of this book, we are interested in *residential* intentional communities. Places where people choose to live in relatively close proximity to each other as a community.

There is a huge diversity of types of residential intentional communities within this umbrella term. Or if we flip that metaphor, intentional community is a big basket holding many unique flowers expressing different ways we can reimagine life together.

A group house. A cohousing neighborhood. A rural ecovillage with gardens and solar panels. A land trust. A Christian farm. A senior cohousing development. A cooperative apartment building. An income-sharing commune. A spiritual retreat center where people live year-round.

All are real examples of intentional communities.

So, working definition:

An intentional community is a group of people who choose to live together (or near each other) in an ongoing way, with some shared purpose, shared values, and shared agreements about how they live.

Let's slow that down.

"Choose to live together." This isn't just "we all happen to rent in the same apartment complex because it was cheaper." People are actively choosing one another as neighbors.

"Ongoing way." This isn't just a retreat weekend or a summer camp. We're talking about people building daily life together.

"Shared purpose." There's a reason they're doing it. It might be sustainability, the arts, mutual care, affordability, spiritual practice, raising kids in a village, aging with dignity, or simply wanting deep human connection. Often communities have *explicit* shared values that codify their purpose.

"Shared agreements." People in intentional communities don't just "hope it works out." They create systems to foster cooperative living. Who cooks dinner on Thursdays. How much noise is okay after 10 p.m. How decisions get made. How someone becomes a member. Where money goes.

Some communities are very structured and formal. Others are more loose and voluntary. But they're all intentional in the sense that people are actively co-creating a shared way of life.

How Intentional Communities Form

Most communities begin with the same general idea: life would be better done together.

Sometimes the idea starts with a small group of friends talking around a kitchen table. Other times it begins with one person who already has land and decides they do not want to live there alone. Other times an existing farm, permaculture project, or nonprofit gets the notion to add-on a residential community.

From there, earnest work begins. These "burning souls" meet regularly. They talk about values, write down agreements, possibly raise money, look for land or develop what they have, talk to banks and lawyers, sort out permits, sketch buildings, and figure out how decisions will be made. Some groups renovate existing houses or farm buildings. Others build from the ground up. Everyone learns quickly that community is as much about spreadsheets and budgets as it is heart circles and talking sticks.

It is important to say that this stage can take a long time. This is the purgatory of the "potluck stage." Many groups never get to land. Some founders find that once the excitement wears off, the details feel overwhelming. Others get far along only to discover that the culture is not strong enough to hold the stress or financial risk of building something together. Starting a community is hard. It asks you to be patient, organized, flexible, and willing to learn as you go.

Still, people choose to do it. All over the world, someone is planting fruit trees for future neighbors or showing a friend a piece of land and saying, "Can you imagine what we could build here?" Every thriving community you will ever visit began with a few people who believed that living cooperatively was worth the effort and who kept going when the work got real.

A Very Old Idea with a Modern Face

Intentional community is not a 1960s invention. It is not a new "alternative lifestyle," either. Communal living organized around shared values is as old as humanity itself.

For most of human history, people lived in close-knit villages, clans, and kinship networks where land, labor, and childcare were shared. Many Indigenous and traditional cultures around the world continue to live this way today. These *unintentional intentional communities* are not born from trend or ideology, but from an unbroken lineage of interdependence.

"In African villages, we do not hold debates about what a community is because we are too busy living as a community! Also, we have a larger definition than most people in the West understand. Our community not only includes the people near and far, but also nature and the land of our ancestors!" writes Jacky Yenga in *ReInhabiting the Village*.

Recorded examples of intentional communities stretch back millennia. One of the earliest documented examples in Western history appears around 525 BCE with Homakoeion, a vegetarian communal settlement in southern Italy. Monastic traditions across many religions created structured communal life rooted in shared labor, values, and spiritual practice. In the 1800s, the United States saw hundreds of utopian experiments—Shaker villages, abolitionist homesteads, Quaker settlements, and cooperative farms—while Europe gave rise to movements such as the Eden cooperative in Germany and Tolstoyan communities inspired by land-based simplicity and shared ethics.

After the world wars, new communities emerged in response to trauma and a deep longing for peace and social rebuilding. The Bruderhof grew from roots in Germany, Taizé in France became a beacon of reconciliation, and kibbutzim flourished in Israel as models of shared land, work, and childcare. Gandhi-inspired ashram communities in India blended land stewardship, spirituality, and social justice.

Then came the 1960s and '70s. Across North America and Europe, young people left mainstream society for communes, land trusts, feminist collectives, and back-to-the-land homesteads. Many of these experiments did not last—and some absolutely did. Several "hippie-era" communities are still alive today, including Twin Oaks in Virginia (founded 1967), The Farm in Tennessee (founded 1971), and Miccosukee Land Co-op in Florida (founded 1973).

In recent decades, ecovillages, cohousing neighborhoods, regenerative farms, and community land trusts have emerged around the world—from Denmark's Christiania and Iceland's Sólheimar, to Sarvodaya ecovillages in Sri Lanka and rural communities across Latin America and Africa.

As these movements matured, organizations arose to support, document, and connect them.

The founding of the Fellowship of Intentional Communities in 1949 was inspired by Arthur E. Morgan to connect and support communal settlements in the United States. In the mid 1980s, the organization became the Fellowship for Intentional Community, and today the Foundation for Intentional Community (FIC) operates as a nonprofit resource hub for people joining, building, and learning about intentional communities.

And in the early 1970s, *Communities* magazine emerged as a central publication for sharing stories from communities themselves, helping document the movement as it evolved.

Internationally, the Global Ecovillage Network (GEN) formed in the 1990s to connect ecovillages and community initiatives across continents.

Today, GEN operates across five global regions and includes numerous regional and national networks, sharing knowledge on sustainability, governance, and cultural resilience.

Scholarly research on communal living has also been supported by organizations such as the International Communal Studies Association (ICSA), first convened in 1985 to bring together people studying intentional communities across cultures and history.

Since around the 1990s, the Cohousing Association of the United States has played a key role in advancing cohousing as a viable and increasingly mainstream housing model. Similar cohousing networks have emerged in the UK and Canada.

Together, these organizations—and many more not listed here—have helped transform scattered experiments into a visible, interconnected movement.

Today's movement includes communities that feel far closer to the mainstream than the countercultural enclaves that defined earlier generations. Cohousing neighborhoods in suburbs. Senior cohousing as an alternative to nursing homes. Agrihoods organized around working farms. Interfaith spiritual communities. Urban cooperative households. Rural projects with nonprofit ownership to preserve long-term affordability. Most of these are models you could explain to your parents.

In other words, community is no longer just "a bunch of twenty-somethings on a commune in the woods." It is showing up in cities, in retirement planning, in real estate development, in climate resilience work, in housing affordability conversations, and in disability care networks.

Some communities are openly radical. Some are quietly practical. Some look like ordinary neighborhoods, plus dinner together twice a week.

All of that counts.

Cooperative Culture vs. Default Culture

Yana Ludwig, in *The Cooperative Culture Handbook*, describes cooperative culture as a set of practices that support belonging, emotional maturity, transparency, skill-building, and the ability to stay in relationship even when things get messy. She writes that communities often fail not because they lack idealism or vision, but because they lack **the cultural tools** to work through the everyday friction of being human together.

Most of us were raised inside **competitive culture**. It sounds like:

- "I win, you lose."
- "My property, my rules."
- "Don't tell me what to do."
- "Mind your own business."
- "If there's a problem, call the police or a lawyer."

This operating system shapes almost everything in mainstream society: power is centralized, conflict is adversarial, and individual freedom is prioritized over collective well-being.

Cooperative culture runs on a fundamentally different logic. It says:

- "Let's figure this out together so it works for everyone."
- "Your experience matters to me even if I don't agree yet."
- "When there's tension, we face it and move through it."
- "We pool resources when possible, instead of hoarding them."

As one community elder put it: *In mainstream culture, difference is a threat. In cooperative culture, difference is information.*

This shift in mindset is part of why intentional communities matter far beyond the people who live in them. They become living laboratories for how humans might share power, manage conflict, and meet needs in ways that are both compassionate and functional.

Intentional communities are not utopias. They are very human places where financial stress, personality clashes, grief, burnout, and even world events show up in microcosm.

The difference is that in community, we choose to face those challenges together instead of alone. We get to practice new ways of being. We can practice hearing instead of reacting, collaborating instead of competing, repairing instead of retreating. Community doesn't remove difficulty; it gives us a space to build the muscles we need to meet it with courage, compassion, and creativity.

And every time a group of people learns to stay in relationship through conflict, or to solve a problem by turning toward one another rather than away, we take one small step toward a more cooperative world.

I once lived in a community in Slovenia with a simple example of cooperative culture. Most meals were cooked communally and eaten together. Whatever food couldn't be produced in the gardens was ordered in bulk or purchased from the city shops. Yet no one was ever asked for grocery money.

Instead, we had the *magic jar*.

This humble mason jar hung in the center of the kitchen, watched over by a paper-mâché kitchen spirit. Loose change, kind offerings from visitors, a bit of unexpected income—anything and everything found its way, anonymously, into that jar.

When we needed money for food, the money was always there.

To my knowledge, that system never failed. The jar never ran dry. And the community is still well fed to this day, thanks to good cooperation and a kindly kitchen spirit.

How Many Are We Talking?

People always ask, "So…how many are there?" It's hard to pin down an exact number, because many communities don't advertise themselves publicly and many exist in forms that don't fit neat categories.

The Foundation for Intentional Community (FIC) has estimated that there are likely tens of thousands of intentional communities worldwide in some form, from small, informal groups to large, long-running villages. If we were to include religious groups that live together within residential communities, such as monasteries, that number would be closer to hundreds of thousands.

One of my hopes with this book is that it may inspire scholarly inclined readers to pursue research into intentional communities. We certainly need more documentation of the modern intentional communities movement, especially to better understand its current scale and growth.

Perhaps the largest non-religious intentional community is Auroville, located in southern India. This community is known as the City of Dawn, home to over 3,000 people from all corners of the globe striving to realize human unity and live in alignment with higher consciousness. In the United States, the largest ecovillage is Ecovillage at Ithaca in upstate New York, with hundreds of residents, multiple neighborhoods, and over 90% of its 175 acres in gardens, farms, and preserved habitat.

There are regional networks of communities, as well as networks based on type and mission. For example, Camphill is a network of more than 100 communities in 20 countries, that are designed for people with and without special needs to live together. In my home state of Vermont, we have a growing network of intentional communities, about 20 throughout the state, that meet regularly and maintain an email listserv for mutual support. Europe has a highly organized network of ecovillages, structured according to national and regional affiliation, with an annual summer conference taking place in a different community each year.

Of course, most intentional communities are much smaller in size than the examples above and many are not (yet) as well networked. Still, it can be surprising for someone new to the concept to learn just how much is happening within our blossoming subculture of intentional community living!

Now that you understand what we mean by "intentional community," we're going to get more specific.

In the next chapter, we'll explore different community models—cohousing, ecovillages, income-sharing communes, spiritual communities, senior communities, cooperative neighborhoods, tiny house villages, and more. You'll see what they actually look like, how they function, what daily life feels like, and which models might fit *you*.

TYPES OF INTENTIONAL COMMUNITIES

> "Intentional community has developed in our Western culture as a means of trying out new social forms, based on the idea that we can create or design social patterns rather than just inheriting them."
> —Jan Martin Bang, *Growing Eco-Communities*

By now you've seen why people are seeking community, and you've seen what we even mean by "intentional community." The next question most people ask is:

"Okay, but what does it actually look like in real life?"

This is where things can get confusing, because communities call themselves all kinds of things: ecovillage, cohousing, commune, housing co-op, coliving, tiny house village, Camphill, Catholic Worker, kibbutz, land trust, and on and on.

It's easy to get lost in the vocabulary.

This chapter gives you a map.

We're going to walk through the most common types of intentional communities you'll hear about. You'll see how they tend to work, who they tend to attract, and what daily life in each one *feels* like.

Two important notes before we dive in:

1. These are patterns, not rigid boxes.

    Communities don't always fit neatly in one category. You'll find "tiny house ecovillages." You'll find "senior cohousing." You'll find spiritual communities that are also farming collectives that are also cooperatives. Even communities that misuse or make up names for themselves.

2. The label is not the community.

    You cannot assume that "ecovillage" means off-grid, or that "cohousing" means friendly, or that "commune" means what you think it means. You still have to dig into their values, go meet the people, walk the land.

There's an expression in the communities movement: If you've seen one community, *you've seen one community.* Each one is unique. Still, there are some common types you're likely to encounter when browsing community directories. I've focused here on models with distinct terminology and established networks so you can move into your research with clearer language and expectations.

Cohousing

What it is:
Cohousing is one of the most approachable and mainstream forms of intentional community.

First described by architects Katie McCamant and Charles Durrett while studying the model in Denmark in the '70s, cohousing has now spread around the world. The Cohousing Association of the United States (CohoUS) estimates there are 200 cohousings established in the United States today, with at least that many in some stage of development.

People often assume "cohousing" means people sharing a house together, but that's quite the opposite of what the term means.

In cohousing, each household owns a private home (or condo/apartment/townhouse). You have your own kitchen, bathroom, and front door. In addition, there are shared common spaces that everyone co-owns and helps manage: a common house usually with a big kitchen and dining area for shared meals, guest rooms, kids' play areas, workshop, perhaps a laundry room.

People often eat together a few nights a week. Cars are parked on the periphery for safer pedestrian paths. There are work days where everyone tends the grounds or maintains shared infrastructure. Decisions are made together. You actually know your neighbors.

Who it tends to attract:
People who want connection and a lighter environmental footprint, but who still want their own fully independent unit. Cohousing is also very popular for aging in community, because it allows elders to keep autonomy while not being isolated.

Costs:
Since they are based on homeownership and often constructed with a developer, cohousing is one of the most expensive community living options, with homes at or even above market rate (remember you are buying into much more than just a house). Occasionally cohousings have rental or subsidized housing opportunities.

Snapshot example:
Heartwood Cohousing in Colorado is one of the largest cohousings by land acreage, yet the homes are clustered near each other with shared parking to foster social connection and keep hundreds of acres accessible to all, including wildlife. (It's the opposite of conventional rural development, where land is carved into private lots and shared access is lost.)

Ecovillages

What it is:
Simply put, "ecovillage" refers to a type of intentional community that focuses on sustainability and regeneration.

The concept builds on many early ecologically-minded communities, eventually popularized by Robert and Diane Gilman in a 1991 report. Then the first major ecovillage conference in 1995 led to the founding of the Global Ecovillage Network (GEN). To date, GEN estimates there are more than 10,000 ecovillages worldwide.

Many beautiful definitions have arisen to describe an ecovillage:

> "human-scale full-featured settlement in which human activities are harmlessly integrated into the natural world in a way that is supportive of healthy human development, and can be successfully continued into the indefinite future."
> —ROBERT GILMAN

> "intentional or traditional communities, consciously designed through participatory process to regenerate their social and natural environments."
> —KOSHA JOUBERT

"any community striving to live high quality and low impact lifestyles."
—Daniel Greenberg

You can expect to find permaculture gardens, solar panels, rainwater catchment, strawbale homes, and perhaps composting toilets at ecovillages. However, don't expect to find communities that are 100% self-sufficient or off-grid. As Kosha Joubert says, "an ecovillage is a process, not an outcome." In fact, many communities aren't striving for complete independence in their food or energy. They're aiming for **interdependence**—partnering with neighbors, strengthening local systems, and reducing reliance on distant resources. Some ecovillages, like Los Angeles Ecovillage in California, are right in the middle of cities, focusing on how to live more sustainably within existing urban buildings.

Who it tends to attract:
People who want to live more lightly on the planet, who want to be part of building solutions, and who are often interested in self-reliance, food systems, land connection, resilient infrastructure, and alternative governance.

Costs:
Prices can vary widely as ecovillages utilize many different legal structures and ownership models. Rental and self-built homes are more common. Some are expensive to join like the high-end luxury ecovillages, especially in expat destinations like Costa Rica or Bali. While others are super affordable, often located in remote regions with no building code enforcement like Dancing Rabbit Ecovillage in Missouri.

Snapshot example:
Earthaven Ecovillage in North Carolina had spent decades refining land stewardship practices, off-grid power, and cooperative decision-making. So when Hurricane Helene tore through the region in 2024—flooding

towns, knocking out power, and displacing thousands—Earthaven came through relatively unscathed, even with the capacity to help surrounding neighbors.

Housing Cooperatives (Co-ops)

What it is:
Perhaps you are familiar with a food or energy coop. Well, a housing coop takes the same legal structure and applies it to the home.

In a housing co-op, residents collectively own and govern the housing where they live. Instead of paying rent to an outside landlord, they become members of a cooperative and participate in decisions about cost, maintenance, culture, and membership. The housing is typically a room within a shared home, although full apartments and stand-alone homes are possible.

Some are multi-household networks spread across a city. Some operate like long-term shared housing with an explicit social mission. Some co-ops are student- or youth-oriented (look into NASCO, North American Students of Cooperation).

Who it tends to attract:
People who want affordability, shared governance, and stability without needing to buy a single-family home alone. Also common among people who care about democratic control of housing and protection from exploitative landlords.

Costs:
Cooperatives tend to function on a "rental" basis, with monthly payments contributed towards the collective. The rent is often much lower than

surrounding prices, with some explicitly intended to create affordability, such as the network of co-op houses in Wisconsin with the Madison Community Cooperative or in Colorado with the Boulder Housing Coalition.

Snapshot example:
Queen City Cooperative in Denver, Colorado was cofounded by Sarah Wells, a cooperative real estate agent on a mission to seed cooperatives throughout the city. Her work also aims to help shift outdated zoning rules that limit the number of unrelated adults who can live together—laws originally designed to exclude poor and marginalized communities.

Shared Housing / "Group House"

What it is:
Multiple unrelated adults living together in one home or a set of connected units, sharing kitchen, common space, sometimes vehicles, sometimes finances. You'll also hear terms like homesharing, cohouseholding, intentional house, commoning.

Sometimes this is informal. Sometimes it's extremely intentional, with written agreements, chore systems, financial transparency, house culture, guest policies, and conflict processes.

Who it tends to attract:
People who want immediate community and affordability without buying property. This is especially common in college towns, activist circles, arts communities, urban environments, and among people in their 20s and 30s. Also increasingly common for single adults in midlife and elders who do not want to live alone.

Snapshot example:
The National Shared Housing Resource Center is a network of independent nonprofit homesharing programs across the United States and an excellent resource for finding a homeshare arrangement that may be a fit for you. While not a full-fledged intentional community, this model is a great starting point for overcoming loneliness and trying out living with others.

Coliving

What it is:
Coliving is a newer housing model allowing lots of mobility; it grew out of coworking culture and the rise of remote work. Residents rent furnished rooms or micro-units inside a larger shared building with communal kitchens, lounges, and coworking areas. Some companies operate global networks, allowing you to move between cities under one membership.

It's important to note that coliving is **not intentional community in the deeper sense**. Residents rarely co-own property or participate in collective decision-making. The model is designed for convenience and built-in social life rather than long-term, self-governed community.

Who it tends to attract:
Remote workers, digital nomads, creatives, and professionals in transition. Coliving works best for adults who want instant social connection without long leases. Most spaces are not set up for families, and many do not allow children.

Cost:
Coliving tends to be more affordable than renting a studio apartment in the same neighborhood, but more expensive than cooperative housing or sharing a house. You're partly paying for flexibility, furnished spaces,

and a ready-made social environment. Most leases include utilities, Wi-Fi, cleaning of common areas, and access to shared amenities, which can simplify budgeting.

Snapshot example:
Outsite, a global coliving network, offers furnished rooms and coworking space in locations like Santa Cruz, California. Members can stay for a month, then hop to another Outsite location—Lisbon, Bali, Mexico City—under a single membership. It's a convenient, low-commitment way to experience community-oriented living.

Spiritual or Religious Communities

What it is:
These are communities organized around a shared spiritual or religious path. They can look like monasteries, ashrams, meditation centers, interfaith retreat centers, Christian or Jewish villages, or Sufi houses. Daily life often includes shared practices such as prayer, meditation, ritual, chanting, shared meals, and forms of service. Most have a strong sense of shared purpose.

Experiences vary widely. Some communities are deeply nourishing and grounded. Others can become overly hierarchical or controlling. Visit in person, ask clear questions, and trust your instincts. Many run retreat centers, which makes it easy to stay for a workshop or silent retreat before considering a longer commitment.

Who it tends to attract:
People who want their spiritual life woven into everyday routines. Seekers who feel drawn to discipline, shared practice, and a sense of meaning. Families sometimes choose these communities because they want children raised within a faith-centered culture.

Costs:
Costs range from simple, low-fee living arrangements with work contributions to retreat-style programs with higher fees. A few communities require vows or long-term commitments. Always look closely at financial expectations, labor requirements, and how authority works.

Snapshot example:
The Lama Foundation in New Mexico hosts a small resident community rooted in daily practice, shared meals, and service. Members often say, "Community is the teacher," reflecting their belief that spiritual growth happens through everyday relationships and shared life.

Tiny House Villages

What it is:
Tiny house villages are clusters of small dwellings on shared land, often organized around communal facilities like a shared kitchen, bathhouse, community room, garden, or tool shed. Some are grassroots projects created by friends who want to live simply, keep costs down, and avoid full-size mortgages. Others are intentionally built as supportive, long-term housing for people emerging from homelessness.

The model varies widely—from resident-owned cooperatives to nonprofit-run villages—but the core idea stays the same: modest private space paired with meaningful shared space. Many villages are listed in directories such as **ChooseTiny.com**, which catalogs community-oriented tiny house settlements across the country.

Who it tends to attract:
People focused on affordability, minimalism, or reduced environmental footprint. Older adults looking to age in place with a supportive, walkable

village around them. Folks who value privacy in their own small unit but also want neighbors close enough to borrow sugar or share a garden bed. And of course, people who simply love tiny homes.

Costs:
Costs range from very low (in nonprofit or transitional villages) to moderate (in resident-owned cooperatives or privately run villages). Residents typically pay a monthly fee that covers land lease, shared utilities, and community facilities. Some communities offer paths to partial ownership or shared equity, while others remain rental-based.

Snapshot example:
SquareOne Villages in Eugene, Oregon develops tiny house and small-home communities designed as permanently affordable, community-owned housing. Residents live in compact, energy-efficient dwellings and collectively govern shared spaces, creating an affordable village model rooted in stability and dignity.

Senior Communities / Senior Cohousing

What it is:
These are communities created for older adults, often age 55 or 60 and up. Some are built using the cohousing model, with private homes and shared common spaces. Others function more like cooperatives or small, informal neighborhoods. The shared goal is simple: to age in community rather than in isolation or in an institution.

Senior communities tend to prioritize accessibility, mutual support, shared transportation, shared meals, and plenty of social connection. This is one of the fastest-growing areas of intentional community, with groups like SAGE Senior Cohousing Advocates helping people create elder-friendly neighborhoods designed for real quality of life.

Who it tends to attract:
People who are clear that they do not want to spend their later years alone in a single-family house in a car-dependent suburb. Instead of choosing to join a multigenerational community that may or may not have the capacity to support aging in place, they want to live in a community where it is possible to age with friendship, safety, and purpose.

Costs:
Costs vary widely. Some senior cohousing communities involve purchasing a home, similar to a small condo. Others use cooperative ownership structures that lower the cost of entry. A few offer rental or mixed-income options. In most cases, shared resources help reduce overall expenses for residents.

Snapshot example:
Village Hearth Cohousing in North Carolina is an LGBTQ+ affirming senior cohousing community designed by and for its residents. The homes and common spaces prioritize accessibility, safety, companionship, and the kind of daily support older adults often cannot find in traditional senior housing.

Communes / Income-Sharing Communities

What it is:
When people hear the word *commune*, they often picture the 1960s: flower crowns, free love, little structure. But "commune" is actually an economic term. It simply means a group of people who choose to share income and resources. And today, only a small percentage of intentional communities use this model. Most communities keep finances separate.

Income-sharing communities operate differently. Members pool most or all of their income or labor into a common economy. In return, the community covers basic needs such as housing, food, transportation, and even healthcare access. Decisions tend to be egalitarian, with a strong emphasis on transparency and shared responsibility. Daily work is also shared. Instead of everyone having one job, members often rotate through essential roles so labor is distributed fairly.

It is a unique way of living. It requires trust, cooperation, and a willingness to participate fully in shared life. Yet for people who feel drained by the competitive, individualistic mainstream economy, this model can be deeply freeing. The Federation of Egalitarian Communities is a network of groups living this way today.

Who it tends to attract:
People who want an alternative to the "every person for themselves" economy. Often idealists who are comfortable with deep sharing and genuinely interested in trying a different way of living.

Costs:
Many income-sharing communities do not require any buy-in. New members usually contribute their income or work within community businesses. Some communities ask that outside assets be held separately during membership to maintain economic equality.

Snapshot example:
Kommune Niederkaufungen in Germany is one of the largest and most stable income-sharing communities in Europe. Founded in 1986, it continues to operate with shared income, cooperative labor, and a strong commitment to egalitarian culture.

Camphill and Other Care-Based Communities

What it is:
Camphill is a global network of intentional communities where people with and without disabilities live, work, and create daily life together. These communities are usually rural and emphasize meaningful work, land stewardship, craft, community arts, and shared daily rhythms. L'Arche communities share a similar spirit and commitment to mutual care.

These are not facilities. They are real communities rooted in dignity, contribution, and interdependence.

There are newer branches of care-based community models that bring together a variety of groups in ways that benefit all. For example, Treehouse Communities in Massachusetts bring foster families and older adults together to create a supportive, intergenerational neighborhood. Care-based models echo the Camphill and L'Arche ethos of creating a community where everyone has something to give and something to receive.

Who it tends to attract:
People drawn to service, caregiving, and relational living. Families seeking an inclusive environment for a loved one with special needs. Individuals who want daily life to feel purposeful and human-centered. Elders who want to contribute meaningfully. Parents and caregivers looking for a supportive, intergenerational setting.

Costs:
Costs vary. Many Camphill communities rely on volunteers and offer room, board, and training in exchange for service. Long-term residents sometimes contribute modestly depending on their role, needs, and structure. Intergenerational communities like Treehouse often follow affordable housing or mixed-income models.

Snapshot example:
Camphill Village Copake in upstate New York is one of the oldest and best-known examples. Residents live in household groups, share meals, work on the land or in craft workshops, and create a vibrant, interdependent culture together.

Kibbutzim and Kibbutz-Inspired Communities

What it is:
The kibbutz is one of the most influential intentional community models in the world. Originating in Israel in the early 1900s, kibbutzim were built on collective ownership, agriculture, shared labor, and a strong ethic of mutual responsibility.

Over the decades many have partially privatized, yet the core principles and ideals now extend far beyond Israel.

Across the world you'll find Jewish intentional communities and diaspora groups borrowing from the kibbutz model: cooperative land stewardship, shared ritual and holiday life, communal childcare, collective security, and a strong sense of cultural continuity. These communities blend tradition with experimentation, creating modern versions of village life grounded in shared identity.

Who it tends to attract:
People who want their economic, social, and cultural life interwoven. Those with a strong Jewish cultural identity, families seeking shared childcare and ritual life, and people drawn to cooperative structures with a clear sense of mission.

Costs:
Costs vary widely. Some communities operate on standard housing and membership fees. Others use cooperative or partially collective financial models. Many offer sliding scales or work-exchange options depending on the structure.

Snapshot example:
Hakhel is a global network that supports new and emerging Jewish intentional communities. Their member groups range from urban cooperative households to rural farms and multigenerational villages that blend Jewish practice with communal living.

Catholic Worker and Other Service-Based Communities

What it is:
Catholic Worker communities, inspired by the work of Dorothy Day and Peter Maurin, combine intentional living with direct service. Many operate houses of hospitality, small farms, soup kitchens, food distribution programs, healing spaces, or safe housing for people who would otherwise be unhoused or in danger. Daily life blends shared meals, prayer or reflection, simple living, and solidarity with those on the margins.

These are not charities with staff. They are communities. People live together, work together, and extend hospitality from their own homes. Although rooted in Catholic tradition, many Catholic Worker communities welcome people of any or no religious background. Similar patterns exist in Quaker service communities, where the shared ethos matters more than formal affiliation.

Who it tends to attract:
People motivated by justice work and radical hospitality. Those who want their spiritual or ethical values reflected in daily life. Individuals who feel called to serve and to live close to those most affected by inequality.

Costs:
Varies widely. Many communities provide room and board for committed members who contribute significant service. Some are donation supported. Financial expectations are usually low, although emotional and labor commitments can be high.

Snapshot example:
White Rose Catholic Worker Farm in Missouri integrates hospitality, land-based living, and spiritual practice. Residents grow food, support people in crisis, and create a home that blends service with community life.

Resident-Owned Communities (ROCs)

What it is:
Resident-Owned Communities are neighborhoods of manufactured or mobile homes where the residents collectively purchase the land beneath their houses and manage it as a cooperative. Instead of renting lots from an outside park owner who can raise rents or sell the property, residents become their own landlord. This model has become one of the strongest affordability and housing-security strategies in North America, especially for low- and fixed-income households. ROC USA is the leading organization helping residents organize, finance, and purchase their parks so they can take control of their housing future.

Who it tends to attract:
Working-class families, seniors on fixed incomes, rural and small-town residents, and anyone who has experienced the insecurity of "owning the home but not the land." Many people join ROCs because they want stability, democratic control, and a community where neighbors look out for one another.

Costs:
Monthly cooperative dues, which tend to be far more stable and predictable than typical lot rents. Members also buy a small equity share in the cooperative. Costs vary by region and by what the community needed to borrow to purchase the land.

Snapshot example:
Sterling View Cooperative in Vermont is a resident-owned manufactured home community where neighbors collectively manage the property, set fair lot fees, and protect long-term affordability. Instead of facing the uncertainty of an absentee landlord, residents decide together how their community operates.

Community-Led Initiatives and Transition-Style Projects

What it is:
Not all intentional communities take the form of villages or shared houses. Some grow out of ordinary neighborhoods where people decide they want something better for the place they already live. Community-led initiatives (often called CLIs in Europe) are grassroots efforts where residents organize around climate resilience, mutual aid, and local decision-making. In other

regions these efforts go by names like Transition Towns or regenerative neighborhood projects.

People may not share land or housing, yet they behave like a community. They form working groups, host shared meals, organize gardens, create emergency plans, run neighborhood time banks, or launch nonprofits that serve the local area. These projects are part of the same movement toward cooperative culture. They simply begin from the block level rather than from a shared property.

Networks like ECOLISE in Europe and the global Transition Town movement support thousands of these efforts around the world.

Who it tends to attract:
People who want community but cannot or do not want to relocate. Residents who want to improve their own neighborhood. People who look around and think, "We could make this place stronger, safer, greener, and more connected if we worked together."

Costs:
Usually low or volunteer-based. Some projects secure grants, shared funds, or municipal partnerships. Most rely on local contributions, sweat equity, or cooperative fundraising.

Snapshot example:
The Dudley Street Neighborhood Initiative in Massachusetts shows what is possible when residents organize for the well-being of their neighborhood. Over several decades they have created community gardens, protected land through a community land trust, strengthened housing stability, and built the kind of local democracy many people wish they had where they live.

And Beyond

The list doesn't stop here. You will also find:

- Artist and activist collectives
- Community land trusts (a nonprofit model for affordable housing)
- Veterans' intentional communities
- Agrihoods (neighborhoods organized around shared agriculture)
- Re-entry communities for people coming out of incarceration
- Decentralized Autonomous Organization (DAO) communities experimenting with crypto-enabled governance
- Communities explicitly for BIPOC or neurodivergent individuals
- Rural retreat centers where a core group lives full-time and stewards the space
- Pocket neighborhoods (small clusters of cottages around shared space)
- Anastasia communities inspired by the Ringing Cedar books
- Low-EMF, off-grid, and homesteading communities
- Indigenous and traditional villages practicing long-standing communal lifeways, which in many cases predate and inform everything we're talking about here

How to Use These Categories

You don't have to memorize this list.

The point is not to turn you into an expert in terminology. The point is to help you start noticing patterns so you can narrow your search.

A few tips for working with this information:

- Notice what energizes you. As you read these descriptions, did one of them make you feel some relief in your body? Pay attention to that.
- Don't get hypnotized by the label. Two places might both call themselves "ecovillages," and one could feel like home while the other feels like a cult. You still have to visit.
- Be honest about how much shared life you actually want. Are you thrilled by the idea of shared meals three nights a week? Or does that feel suffocating and you'd rather have "wave to neighbors and occasionally potluck" levels of contact?
- Think about phase of life. A community that's magical for a retired couple might not work for a single parent of a toddler, and vice versa. Senior cohousing can be paradise for aging with dignity. A fast-moving coliving house might be perfect for a 28-year-old designer who works remotely and wants community in a new city.
- Ask: "Is this model financially realistic for me?" Some models are ownership-based. Some are rental-based. Some require buy-ins. Some require labor instead of money. It matters.

If you want a quick, fun way to start narrowing down the types of communities that might fit you, try the quiz at **communityfinders.com/quiz**. Many people say it gives them their first "aha" moment about what they're actually looking for.

This is also where support helps. Many people try to figure all of this out alone and get overwhelmed fast. A big part of my work is helping people identify which models are a true match for their needs and then pointing them toward specific communities to visit.

That's where we're headed next: clarifying what you want and learning how to visit real communities.

PART II:

DISCOVERING YOUR PATH

ENVISIONING YOUR COMMUNITY FUTURE

> "If one advances confidently in the direction of his dreams, and endeavors to live the life which he has imagined, he will meet with a success unexpected in common hours."
>
> —Henry David Thoreau

Opening Reflection

The key to finding your community is first being honest about what you're searching for.

You may still be at the beginning of all this, just learning what kinds of communities exist—which means you're in the perfect place to dream!

What is the life you want in community? What would your ideal day be like? What's the fantasy vision tucked behind your practical considerations?

Don't worry about realism right now. We'll get grounded soon enough. For now, imagine freely. Later we will bring that dream down to earth.

Before I found my home community, I spent months honing my inner vision. Eventually this vision became a simple list. I called it my Community Wishlist.

Beautiful gardens. A peaceful atmosphere. Lots of families with children (as I hope to raise a family myself someday). The possibility of building my own house. A location in Vermont or the Northeast. A pond. And a sauna to survive the long winters.

The community I eventually joined checked nearly all the boxes.

Interestingly, it didn't have a sauna when I moved in, but one was built later. A good reminder that *you might be the one who brings a missing piece of your vision into the community you eventually call home.*

As Danielle Williams, member of Dancing Rabbit Ecovillage, once shared during a workshop, "Sometimes the thing that you are most missing in a potential community is the thing that you are meant to bring to it."

Before you begin creating your own Community Wishlist, take some time to reflect. Settle into a quiet room or find a sunny spot outdoors. Pour a cup of tea. Pull out your journal. And dream a little.

1 · Starting with Your Why

Every journey toward intentional community begins with a why.

You may already feel your why has taken shape while reading this book.

Maybe you crave connection after years of too much solitude.
Maybe you want to raise your kids in a village setting.
Maybe you desire companionship and support as you age.
Or you want to contribute to something meaningful.

Your why is your compass. It holds steady when the path gets confusing or the search takes longer than expected.

It also prepares you for conversations with communities. "Why do you want to live here?" is often one of the first questions prospective members are asked.

When you name your why, future decisions can come with more ease. You'll have something clear to measure the oncoming opportunities against.

If you're considering starting a community, this clarity becomes even more essential. The possibilities are endless. Your why is what keeps you focused.

Try to move past the surface answers. Ask yourself "why?" again and again until something inside clicks—a deeper longing for belonging, purpose, contribution, or connection. Beneath the practical reasons, there is always a fundamental human desire.

Hold that truth close. It will guide you far better than any checklist.

Write it down.

2 · Clarifying Your Core Values

Once you understand your why, the next step is naming the values beneath it.

Values are the quiet guardrails guiding your choices. They determine why certain communities feel right and others might feel off, even when they look good on paper.

Intentional communities are formed around a set of shared values. Founders establish a purpose, a vision, a way of living, that future members buy into when they join. These values are often displayed boldly on community websites and guiding documents.

How well do you know *your own values*?

If you value self-sufficiency and simplicity, you may be drawn to a rural, off-grid ecovillage. If creativity, diversity, and collaboration matter, a mixed-income urban cohousing group may resonate. If spiritual growth is central, a community built around shared practice might feel like home.

Values evolve over time, but certain ones tend to stay steady: cooperation, celebration, ecological stewardship, joy, autonomy, care for elders, mutual support.

Write down the values that feel most alive for you. They are the ingredients of your future home.

3 · From Values to Vision

Once you know what matters to you, imagine it.

Close your eyes and picture a morning in your ideal community.

What do you hear? Children laughing, roosters crowing, the rustle of someone tending the garden?

Where do you go first? A shared kitchen, a sunny studio, a pond for swimming?

How does your body feel? Relaxed, grounded, energized?

Visioning isn't fantasy. It's felt clarity. Later, when you visit actual communities, you'll be able to sense whether a place reflects the life you've imagined.

I had this experience myself during my first visit to the community I now call home. It was midsummer. Towering sunflowers lined the gardens that kids were racing through in an epic game of capture the flag. My tour guide, a long-time resident, decided it was too hot and suggested a swim. She led me down a woodland path to the most breathtaking pond—spring-fed, huge, with koi gliding just beneath the surface. Everything felt strangely familiar, like déjà vu.

Only later did I realize why: I had envisioned this kind of place before.

Your experience may be different. The community you eventually join may look nothing like the one you imagine today. Life has a way of offering us what we didn't know we needed. Stay open to surprise.

If you have supportive people in your life, ask them, "Where can you imagine me thriving?" Sometimes others see us more clearly than we see ourselves.

Write down or draw an image of what you envision.

4 · Aligning Goals with Values

Values give direction. Goals give motion.

If you've been delaying your community search for too long, now is the time to set some goals. When will you begin visiting communities? When will you reach out? When do you hope to move? When will you share your vision with others?

Put some dates on your calendar.

Your values determine *how* you move toward your goals—with patience, integrity, curiosity, or collaboration. Your goals ensure your values don't stay theoretical.

Sometimes we chase goals that don't honor who we are. We rush, compromise, or say yes when our heart says not yet. When values and goals align, you may feel more flow in your life.

If belonging is your value, your goal might be joining more gatherings or visiting communities this year.

If stewardship is central, you might volunteer with local land projects or attend ecological workshops.

Small, value-aligned steps bring your dream closer even before you relocate anywhere.

5 · Letting Your Vision Evolve

Your vision will shift. That's normal.

Early on, you may picture a tiny, off-grid homestead. Later, you might realize you crave more neighbors and a socially vibrant environment. Or after visiting many communities, you decide to embark on the grand adventure of starting a new community project.

Or, like me, you may eventually realize you take on enough big risky projects in other areas of your life and an established community is the most supportive home for you.

This isn't inconsistency—it's growth.

Keep track of the changes. Each visit, conversation, disappointment, or spark of inspiration adds clarity. Treat your vision as a living document. Revisit it often.

Notice what remains constant even as details shift. The thing that keeps showing up, that's your north.

6 · Carrying the Vision Forward

Envisioning your community future isn't about manifesting a fantasy. It's about knowing yourself well enough to recognize a real possibility when it appears.

The clearer your why, values, and vision, the easier it becomes to sort through options, stay grounded in your decisions, and trust your instincts.

My fiancé, Nathan Oxenfeld, is a natural vision teacher who helps people learn to see without glasses. One of the most surprising things I've learned from him is that eyesight is not always a physical limitation. Often our vision is strained or unclear because our *inner* vision needs development. We need the muscles of imagination, the confidence of self-knowing, and the clarity that comes from feeling in control of our lives in order for our physical sight to improve.

It is a powerful reminder that working on your vision for your future life in community can affect the rest of your being in unexpected ways.

So be open to even more change. Clarity in one area of your life may create more clarity everywhere else.

In the next chapter, we'll take your vision and translate it into tangible criteria.

> **"Tell me, what is it you plan to do
> with your one wild and precious life?"**
> —Mary Oliver

CREATING YOUR COMMUNITY WISHLIST

> "Follow your bliss and the universe will open doors where there were only walls."
>
> —Joseph Campbell

Finding your place in community begins with clarity. After exploring your values and envisioning your ideal future, the next step is to bring those ideas down to earth. A *Community Wishlist* turns vision into form—a living record of what matters most to you as you search for or create a community home.

When you first begin exploring, everything can sound appealing: cob cottages and permaculture farms, urban co-ops buzzing with activism, cohousing neighborhoods with shared gardens and potlucks. Each model has its charm, but not all will meet your needs.

Your Wishlist helps you sort what truly resonates from what sounds good only in theory.

To take this deeper and work through the full exercise, go to **communityfinders.com/book1**. There you'll find the Community Wishlist Worksheet, which guides you step by step.

What the Community Wishlist Is

The Wishlist is both a mirror and a compass: a mirror because it reflects who you are and what you value, and a compass because it points you toward communities most likely to fit.

Creating one doesn't require spreadsheets or long essays. A notebook page will do. The goal is to clarify, not complicate.

Begin by reflecting on a few essentials:

- **Type of community.** What living models call to you—ecovillage, cohousing, shared house, land trust, spiritual center?
- **Location.** What environments help you thrive? Mountains, coastline, countryside, city?
- **Affordability and ownership.** Do you prefer rental, cooperative ownership, or shared finances? What's doable?
- **Size.** Do you imagine a close-knit household or a village-scale network?
- **Culture.** What energy feels right—radical experiment, family-friendly neighborhood, contemplative retreat?
- **Sharing.** How much do you want to share—meals, gardens, income, governance?
- **Governance.** Consensus, sociocracy, or something else?
- **Your role.** What gifts or skills do you bring, and how do you want to participate?
- **Timeline.** When might you realistically move or take your next step?

Take a quiet hour with these questions. Write freely. Don't worry about perfect answers. You're simply sketching the contours of a home that doesn't yet exist on any map.

Turning Reflection into a List

Once your ideas are on paper, distill them into two short lists:

- **Your Top 10 Wishlist** – the qualities you most hope to find in community.
- **Your Top 10 Avoid List** – the situations or dynamics you'd rather not experience.

Once your list is done, the next step is to add a star or highlight the items that are *non-negotiable*—for example, a commitment to ecological living or a particular region. Others can remain *flexible*—nice to have but not essential.

Clarifying your non-negotiables sets your priorities and helps you better communicate them when you reach out to communities.

If you're doing this with a partner or family members, make individual lists first, then compare. Notice where you overlap and where you differ. The conversations you have around your Community Wishlists often reveal what truly matters.

Making and Breaking the Community Wishlist

Since its creation, the Community Wishlist has empowered seekers around the world to approach communities with a clear set of needs in mind.

Yet there's an important caveat:

Community is not a list of items on your shopping list.

Your Wishlist is a *reference tool*, not a set of demands. If you hold it too tightly, you may miss the greatest gift of community—its power to *change you*.

Living with others will stretch you. It asks you to grow into someone more flexible, capable, and generous. Someone who can fill in gaps with your own gifts.

And along the way, you may end up loving aspects of community you never would have put on your Wishlist in the first place. Even something that once sat firmly on your Avoid list can become a surprising gift, especially when it pushes you to grow in ways you didn't expect.

So hold your lists lightly. Let them focus your attention without closing your mind.

Next, we'll look at some of the common types of people drawn to community living, so you can see how your "community type" may fit with existing opportunities.

TYPES OF PEOPLE DRAWN TO COMMUNITY

> "Intentional community is not the buildings and amenities, it's the relationships among the people who live there."
>
> —Laird Schaub

Over the years of helping people find intentional communities, I've spoken with hundreds of clients. Each person has their own story, background, and dream. Some arrive with a crystal-clear vision, while others are still figuring out what "community" even means to them.

And yet, I've noticed a pattern. Though everyone comes from different circumstances, most are walking toward the same destination: a life with more meaning, connection, and belonging.

While those longings are universal, the motivations that bring people to this path vary widely. Over time, I've come to recognize a few recurring types—archetypes, really—of people who find their way to intentional communities.

You may recognize yourself in one (or several) of the archetypes below. Most of us are hybrids and will shift between types over time. As you read, notice where you see yourself: past, present, and future.

1 · The Village Dreamer

You long for a real neighborhood. People who know your name, show up when needed, and share life in simple ways. You want a balance: community without claustrophobia, connection without giving up autonomy.

Practical considerations:

- Cohousing is often an excellent fit.
- Look for communities with private homes and optional shared meals.
- Check if there are shared spaces (common house, gardens, paths) that encourage natural social interaction.
- Ask about social expectations: Do people gather weekly or daily? Is it structured or organic?
- If you're introverted, confirm that quiet spaces and boundaries are respected.

Sound like you? Reflection invitation:
Where in your current life do you feel the absence of village, and what kind of connection do you most want to cultivate?

_____
_____

2 · The Freedom-Loving Homesteader

You want land, a garden, maybe chickens or a workshop. You love independence and the rhythm of working with your hands. But you also know how heavy it is to carry everything alone—the tools, the projects, the upkeep, the isolation. You want to build "self-suffiency" with community.

Practical considerations:

- Ecovillages, rural intentional communities, and permaculture-based projects are ideal.
- Ask how much land is private vs. shared.
- Confirm whether you're allowed to build your own home or modify land.
- Look into water rights, zoning, and community infrastructure.
- Make sure the culture fits your level of desired independence.

Sound like you? Reflection invitation:
What parts of homesteading bring you joy, and which ones feel overwhelming or lonely when you picture doing them alone?

_____

_____

3 · The Spiritual Seeker or Healing Practitioner

You're drawn to places where daily life includes meditation, ritual, prayer, movement, reflection, or shared intention. You want depth, authenticity, and inner growth woven into ordinary life. Perhaps you want a home where people can come to learn and heal alongside you, such as a retreat center.

Practical considerations:

- Visit in person before committing. Spiritual communities vary widely.
- Ask about leadership structures, expectations for participation, and daily rhythms.
- Clarify what "commitment" means: attendance? vows? service hours?
- For healing practitioners, check whether the community has space for your work.
- Make sure the environment feels grounded rather than idealized or controlling.

Sound like you? Reflection invitation:
Which aspects of your spiritual life do you want your home environment to support on a daily basis?

_____

_____

4 · The Digital Nomad or Remote Professional

You love flexibility and mobility, but you're tired of the isolation that can come with it. You want a home base with people—meals, shared workspaces, stimulating conversation—without losing your ability to travel.

Practical considerations:

- Coliving houses or ecovillages with short-term stays are good entry points.

- Research communities that mention "coworking" in their description.
- Check internet quality (a major one!).
- Ask about minimum stay requirements if you prefer mobility.
- For long-term nomads, choose communities used to welcoming newcomers.

Sound like you? Reflection invitation:
What would it feel like to root in one place for a season? What support would make that feel nourishing?

_____

_____

5 · The Conscious Elder

You want to age in place—but not alone. You want companionship, shared meals, mutual support, and neighbors who care whether you're okay. You want dignity and meaningful contribution in your later years.

Practical considerations:

- Senior cohousing is one of the strongest models for aging in community.
- Ask about accessibility design, transportation, and healthcare support.
- Consider if an age-restricted community could work for you.
- If multigenerational, assess whether elders are valued and involved.
- See the later chapter on **Finding Community as an Elder**.

Sound like you? Reflection invitation:
If you could design your later years intentionally, what would daily life look like? Who would be around you?

_____

_____

6 · The Intentional Parent

You want your children to grow up in a true village—with safe play areas, shared childcare, mixed-age friendships, and adults they trust. You want support, not isolation.

Practical considerations:

- Many communities want families with kids, but not all have them (yet!).
- Consider if you could be the pioneers or if you need other kids around already.
- Look for communities with infrastructure for children: play areas, babysitters, education options onsite or nearby.
- Ask how disagreements around parenting are handled.
- See the later chapter on **Raising Children in Community**.

Sound like you? Reflection invitation:
What support do you most want your children (or future children) to experience that is hard to create alone?

_____

_____

7 · The Budget-Mindful Seeker

Your draw to community is equal parts emotional and practical. High rent, rising costs, burnout, or debt have made you wake up to the need for a different model. You want a community that you can both enjoy and afford.

Practical considerations:

- Explore co-ops, ROCs (resident-owned communities), and shared rental communities.
- Consider if income-sharing or work-exchange models are realistic for you.
- Don't get sticker shock, get creative with a prospective community.
- Ask about shared buy-in, subsidized housing, rentals, and lease-to-own options.
- See the later chapter on **How Much Does It Cost?**.

Sound like you? Reflection invitation:
How would your life change if your housing costs were reduced and your support network doubled?

_____

_____

8 · The Transitional Soul

You're in a period of change—burnout, grief, illness, or separation. You know you're not ready to jump into full communal membership, but you can feel that you're not meant to stay where you've been. Perhaps there's a period of healing that can happen within the embrace of community.

Practical considerations:

- Start with low-commitment stays: retreat centers, short-term residencies, working guests, or trial periods.
- Avoid communities with intense expectations until you've regained steadiness.
- Skip the full trauma history in your first message, but be prepared to share more of yourself over time.
- Prioritize emotional safety and clear communication norms.

Sound like you? Reflection invitation:
What kind of environment would help you heal? Stillness? Nature? Gentle structure? Community presence?

_____

_____

9 · The Aspiring Founder

You began this journey looking for a community to join…but somewhere along the way, you realized your ideal community might not exist yet. You're carrying a vision, gathering allies, exploring land, imagining new possibilities.

Practical considerations:

- Visit established communities before you commit to the founder's path.
- If you don't yet have land, focus on building a founding team first.
- Clarify values and governance early.
- Seek training in facilitation, conflict resilience, and cooperative leadership.

- See the later chapter on **Advice for Starting a Community**.

Sound like you? Reflection invitation:
What is the essence of the community you feel called to create? What values or experiences are at its core?

_____

_____

Do you know which type(s) you are? Send me an email to share! Write to me at **cynthia@communityfinders.com**.

Remember, these archetypes aren't boxes to squeeze yourself into. They're starting points that help you recognize what motivates you, what you need, and what you bring to the table. With this clarity, you're better prepared to explore real communities and understand how your personality and priorities shape your search.

In the next chapter, we'll take this reflection further with a self-assessment to help you understand your readiness for community living.

ARE YOU READY FOR COMMUNITY LIVING?

> "Living in community and cohousing specifically is not for everyone and may not be for anyone for their entire lives, but despite the challenges, for me it has proven to be well worth the effort."
>
> —Zev Paiss

A big question you may be sitting with at this point: Am I even ready for community living?

Community living is beautiful, meaningful, life-giving. It can also be messy, slow, and confronting. This chapter is not here to talk you out of community life. It is here to help you know whether now is the right time to pursue it.

Think of this chapter as a gentle reality check. Not a barrier.

The truth is that many communities receive far more inquiries than they can respond to, and too often those messages come from people who are lonely and overwhelmed but not quite ready to step into shared living.

You deserve to know if this is the right moment for you. Communities deserve that too.

Let's take a thoughtful look.

The Community Readiness Checklist

Below is a simple checklist to self-assess your readiness for community living.

You may find that you are strong in some areas and still developing in others. That is completely normal. This list is not meant to discourage you. It is here to help you see where your edges are so that you can grow in ways that support both you and the community you will eventually join.

1 · Openness to Growth and Feedback

Community life involves receiving feedback. Not constant criticism, but gentle course-correcting that helps the group live well together. People may ask for changes in how you manage shared spaces, noise, pets, guests, communication, or participation.

The healthiest communities are the ones where people can speak openly and repair quickly. If you shut down, withdraw, or get defensive in response to feedback, community life may feel stressful. Yet that same stress can also be an invitation to grow. If willing, you can expand your capacity to receive feedback and strengthen your ability to live well with others.

Reflection invitation:
How do I respond when someone points out something I missed or asks me to shift a behavior? Am I open to changing this about myself?

2 · Patience with Meetings and Group Process

Not all communities have long meetings, but some do. Decisions take time. Listening takes time. Reaching agreement takes even more. If you get easily bored, irritable, or frustrated in group settings, community meetings might drain you quickly.

That said, community meetings often look different from the meetings you may be used to. When they are well facilitated and grounded in shared purpose, witnessing a healthy group process can feel surprisingly refreshing—especially for people who say they "don't like meetings."

Reflection invitation:
Can I stay patient and engaged when decisions are slow?

3 · Comfort with Difference

You will not like everyone. You will not agree with everyone. And they will not all agree with you. Community means learning to cooperate with people who see the world differently.

Many communities have lost good people simply because they expected to be surrounded only by like-minded friends. Real communities contain many personalities, opinions, and quirks.

Reflection invitation:
Can I respect and collaborate with people who have different political views, parenting styles, or communication habits?

_____

_____

4 · Flexibility of Vision

You may have a picture of your ideal community. But the community you join will be imperfect, evolving, and not always organized around your dream.

Rigid expectations lead to disappointment. The happiest community members are those who adapt and help create the culture they want, rather than insisting it must already exist.

Reflection invitation:
Can I let go of my ideal vision of what community "should be" in order to appreciate what is actually here?

_____

_____

5 · Willingness to Prioritize Relationships

Community is built on people, not nice scenery. I take a deep breath whenever a client opens with "I want a warm climate" or "somewhere near a beach." Lovely, yes—but the real heart of community is the relationships. I often say, *people matter more than place.*

Focusing only on logistics or location can leave you unprepared for the real work of shared life. When relationships come first, challenges feel more manageable and the rewards greater.

Reflection invitation:
Do I genuinely want to invest time and presence in getting to know the people around me?

___
___

6 · Trust in Group Decisions

An established community will have agreements you did not write. There may even be long-standing decisions you disagree with.

While the nature of participatory decision-making means it's technically possible to change things, rocking the boat isn't always easy or desired. Trusting the wisdom of long-term members is part of community living.

Reflection invitation:
Can I live comfortably with choices I did not personally make?

___
___

7 · Practical Readiness: Time, Energy, Stability

Community life includes work parties, shared meals, meetings, and spontaneous collaboration. It requires a basic level of stability.

People who are in acute crisis, overwhelmed by life, or financially on the edge often struggle to participate fully.

Reflection invitation:
Do I have enough capacity right now to show up as a functioning member?

_____

_____

8 · Emotional Awareness and Personal Responsibility

Community mirrors you back to yourself. You will be triggered. You will frustrate others. You will repair and try again.

People who blame others for all conflict, avoid repair, or resist self-reflection tend to struggle when living in community.

Reflection invitation:
Can I own my part when things get tense, and am I willing to grow?

_____

_____

9 · A Willingness to Slow Down

Community membership is not instant. It is a relationship that needs time, trust, and repeated contact. Plan for 6 months to a year for finding a community fit, and much longer for starting a new community. If you need housing now, prioritize that first and then continue your community search from a grounded place.

Reflection invitation:
Can I let this unfold at its own pace? Is there another housing situation I can find in the meantime as a stepping stone?

_____

_____

Five Tips to Become a Strong Community Candidate

Below are the qualities communities consistently appreciate. Consider them as invitations to grow.

1 · Think Like a Relationship, Not a Transaction

Joining a community is not like applying for a job or buying a house. It is like building relationships with many people at once. Trust, patience, humor, and communication all matter.

Bring curiosity. Ask questions. Be yourself. Send thank you notes. Let connection unfold naturally.

2 · Be Glad When a Community Is Selective

A selective community is one that has learned from experience. Their process protects both sides. Expect interviews, work parties, reading materials, and time. These systems exist so that no one ends up in a place that is not right for them.

3 · Study Up

If a community uses sociocracy, consensus, Nonviolent Communication (NVC), or other specific practices, take time to learn about them. Review their website. Read their agreements. Ask for recommended resources.

Showing initiative demonstrates respect.

4 · Visit Other Communities

Communities trust people who have spent time in other intentional spaces. Visiting helps you understand your own needs far better than research alone.

5 · Work on Yourself

Emotional maturity is one of the most valuable skills you can bring. You do not have to be perfect. You do need to be willing.

Silent walks. Journaling. Therapy. Meditation. Honest conversations. Anything that helps you meet yourself with clarity and compassion will help you meet others that way too.

Red Flags to Address Before You Reach Out

These are not failures. They are signals that you may need more support before diving in.

- You are in acute crisis or grief
- You want community to "fix your life"

- You are looking for a family, not a village
- You expect ideological alignment on everything
- You struggle with boundaries
- You dislike group process
- You want instant belonging
- You feel overwhelmed by responsibilities in your current life

If any of these resonate, take your time. Healing is part of the path.

Green Flags Communities Love to See

These qualities help communities feel confident inviting you in:

- Reliability
- Good communication
- Humility and humor
- Willingness to learn
- Follow-through
- Awareness of your impact
- Skills you're happy to share
- Kindness

You do not need to be exceptional. You only need to be real.

You have just explored an honest look at yourself as a potential community member. This readiness check is not about perfection. It is about self-awareness. The more clearly you know your strengths, your tender spots, and your needs, the more gracefully you will move through the search ahead.

These reflections also help protect communities from being overwhelmed by unprepared inquiries. When you reach out from a place of grounded clarity, both you and the community have a much greater chance of finding a true fit.

In the next chapter, we will build on this self-knowledge by creating something practical: your Community Resume. This will help you communicate who you are, what you offer, and what you are seeking when you begin reaching out to real communities.

You are well on your way.

CREATING YOUR COMMUNITY RESUME

> "Ask not what your community can do for you, but what you can do for your community!"
> —Common saying in the communities movement

Up until now, we've mostly focused on *you*—your motivations, your values, your vision for community life.

Now we shift gears to see things from the community's perspective.

Because as much as you may **long for community**, the communities you'll be reaching out to are wondering something equally important:

Are you who we long for?

Too often I've seen prospective members write to a community with a long list of what they "need." Affordable housing. Childcare. Land to grow food. Support. Healing. Belonging.

All of that is human and understandable. But communities don't want *needy* people. They want *contributing* people—folks who will help their shared home thrive.

Before you start browsing directories or contacting communities, it helps to get clear on what you have to offer. Every intentional community, no matter its size or style, is built on the contributions of its members. When you understand what you bring, you move through this journey with grounded confidence.

This chapter is both a self-assessment tool and a practical resource. A "Community Resume" is not a job resume filled with degrees and titles. It's a snapshot of *who you are in shared life*: your strengths, your skills, your lived experience, and your intentions. You may never send it to anyone or you may use it liberally in your community outreach. Regardless, creating it for yourself is invaluable.

A community resume helps you:

- Recognize the strengths you bring
- Name your limitations honestly
- Identify your work style and relational habits
- Understand the areas where you may need support
- Speak clearly about what you offer when you reach out

Some communities receive dozens of inquiries each week. A thoughtful introduction that includes a clear summary of who you are immediately helps you stand out as prepared, grounded, and considerate.

Once you've created this resume, you'll be able to adapt and add to it as you move through your search. It becomes your calling card and your confidence-builder!

How to Create Your Community Resume

Start with a blank document or use the **Community Resume Worksheet** found at **communityfinders.com/book1**. There you will also find examples of resumes that past clients have made.

Keep it short—one page, ideally with a friendly headshot at the top.

Here's what to include:

1. **Your Past Community Experiences**

   You may not have lived in an intentional community yet, but you've probably participated in some kind of group life—volunteer work, collective housing, teams, or social projects. Include those experiences.

2. **Your Typical Role in Groups**

   How do you naturally show up in community? Are you a quiet worker who keeps things running smoothly? A connector who brings people together? A creative spark? This gives communities a sense of your "relational footprint."

3. **Hard Skills**

   List tangible abilities that would be useful in community life: gardening, construction, fundraising, bookkeeping, cooking, web design, childcare, mediation, teaching, or anything else that supports collective living.

4. **Soft Skills**

   These often matter most. Are you a good listener? Do you facilitate meetings well? Are you patient, adaptable, empathetic, or organized under pressure? Communities thrive on emotional intelligence as much as technical know-how.

5. **Relevant Training or Education**

   Mention workshops or certifications that show your commitment to cooperation and sustainability—such as Nonviolent Communication (NVC), permaculture design, facilitation, or therapy training.

6. **Room for Growth**

    Identify areas where you'd like to grow. Maybe you want to practice clearer communication or learn hands-on skills like carpentry or budgeting. Communities appreciate self-awareness more than perfection.

7. **References (Optional)**

    If you want to go the extra mile, include one to three references. Anyone who can speak to how you contribute to groups (ideally not family members).

Keep the tone humble and friendly. Think of it as an invitation to connection, not a performance.

How to Use It

Once completed, attach your Community Resume when emailing or applying to visit a community. Mention it briefly in your message, such as:

> "I've attached a short community resume that shares a bit more about my background and interests."

That small line communicates professionalism and self-awareness. You can also then keep the body text of your email much shorter, which communities definitely appreciate. You'll be amazed how much more likely you are to receive thoughtful replies.

You can also revisit your resume after each community visit. Update it as you gain new skills or clarity. Many people keep a version just for themselves as a living reflection of their journey.

Phew! You've made it through a big stretch of inner work. You've clarified your motivations, your values, your vision, your strengths, and the gifts you bring. This groundwork matters more than you might realize. With this clarity, you're no longer wandering, you're walking with direction.

Next, we'll take all of this self-knowledge and bring it into the real world. We'll explore how to research communities, how to reach out, how to visit them, and how to evaluate whether a place is a fit. This is where your inner clarity meets lived experience.

Let's keep going.

PART III:

THE SEARCH FOR COMMUNITY

RESEARCHING COMMUNITIES

> "A community is the mental and spiritual condition of knowing that the place is shared, and that the people who share the place define and limit the possibilities of each other's lives. It is the knowledge that people have of each other, their concern for each other, their trust in each other, the freedom with which they come and go among themselves."
>
> —Wendell Berry

This next stage is where your vision starts to meet the real world.

It's also where many people get overwhelmed by long lists, outdated websites, or simply not knowing where to begin. This chapter introduces the tools and strategies for researching intentional communities effectively.

Because websites change and better tools emerge every year, I've created a continually updated resource hub at **communityfinders.com/book1**.

Everything in this chapter is supported (and expanded) there—directories, worksheets, how-to videos, and links I can't keep updated inside a printed book.

Now let's look at the essential research tools to begin your search.

The Key Directories for Finding Communities

There are dozens of intentional community maps and directories online. Most people in North America start with:

- **ic.org/directory**

Maintained by the Foundation for Intentional Community (FIC). This is the most widely used database for those in the United States.

- **cohousing.org/directory**

For US-based cohousing neighborhoods, curated by the Cohousing Association of the United States (CohoUS).

- **ecovillage.org/directory**

For ecovillages around the world through the Global Ecovillage Network (GEN).

There are also a variety of niche directories—tiny house villages, homesteading communities, spiritual communities, elder-focused communities, and more. For example, Diggers and Dreamers maintains a whole directory of intentional communities just in Britain.

Head to **communityfinders.com/book1** to see a complete list with updated links.

Directories are a starting point, not the whole picture. Many small or new communities never register with these databases. Even large, well-established communities can let their listings lapse, so supplement your search with:

- **Basic internet searches** using keywords like "intentional community near [city]," "Vermont cohousing," or "permaculture community Oregon."
- *Communities* **magazine articles** going back decades, with new quarterly issues published online and in print, is a great way to learn

about communities out there, especially if you prefer to spend a bit more time off-screen. Subscribe at **gen-us.net/communities**.
- **Social media groups** such as Facebook's large group "CCCIntentionalCommunities" and regional or topical groups (e.g., "EcoVillages & Communities with Kids Portugal").
- **Word of mouth** through retreats, workshops, flyers hung up in a local cafe, or friends-of-friends who know of group houses or forming projects.

Tools for Choosing a Region

Sometimes finding a community will require relocation. Perhaps you already know the exact region you want to move to. Maybe you're completely open. If you fall anywhere in between, a few research tools can help you compare places before you start reaching out to communities.

A good place to start is **basic affordability**. Even though community living usually lowers expenses through shared resources, the cost of living in a region still matters. A cost-of-living calculator can help you get a realistic sense of what's manageable.

It's also wise to look at **climatic trends**. Weather patterns are shifting, and many areas are experiencing more floods, fires, storms, and water shortages. Interactive climate maps and regional risk charts can help you see how different places may change in the coming decades.

For the more spiritually inclined, **intuitive tools** can also play a role in choosing a region. Some people explore their astrocartography chart, notice synchronicities or recurring dreams connected to certain places, or check systems like Human Design or numerology to understand what environments support their well-being.

If you're considering **moving abroad**, take time to research the ease of visitation, residency, and immigration from your home country. Factor in political stability and how welcoming the culture is toward expats. Several websites now rank countries on expat friendliness, safety, and quality of life, which can help you compare options.

I've gathered all of these at **communityfinders.com/book1**, since websites and maps change over time.

Determining Whether a Community Is Legit

Ever stumble on an amazing community listing, with perfect location and values for you, but a few gaps or quirks leave you scratching your head wondering if this is even real?

Not every "community" listed online is a real, functioning group. Some are one person with a dream. Some sound wonderful but have never gotten past stage one. Others are legitimate but not a match for your needs.

Here are a few practical ways to assess a community's credibility before investing too much time:

Start with their directory listing.

A complete **ic.org** listing, written clearly and updated recently, is a good sign. Consistent spelling, thoughtful descriptions, and a realistic tone show that people are paying attention.

Check their online presence.

Do they have a website? Social media channels? Regular updates? Photos that look real rather than stock images? You're looking for evidence of ongoing life—events, announcements, blog posts, newsletters, land work, celebrations.

Look at the people and the spaces.

Photos should show cared-for spaces and people who look genuinely engaged. No place is perfect, but a healthy community tends to look…well, lived in and loved.

Be wary of overly idealistic language.

If the entire website reads like a manifesto with no practical information—no membership process, no details on governance, no signs of actual residents—proceed slowly. Real communities are aspirational, but they're also grounded in daily life.

For forming communities:
They should clearly state that they are forming, not pretend to be fully established. Look for signs that there is more than one person involved—a team, regular meetings, transparent decision-making, early land plans, or fundraising. Be cautious of "communities" of one or two people unless they are extremely clear about what stage they're in.

If you're still unsure:
Talk to someone who has visited. A personal referral or first-hand account is often the quickest way to know whether a community is stable, grounded, and worth your energy.

Forming vs. Established Communities

As you deepen into your research, you notice that communities tend to fall into two main categories of development: forming and established.

Of course, the community creation process is rarely linear and there are many micro stages involved. Yet it's helpful for you to understand the basic distinction and what it may mean for your engagement.

Forming communities are groups still in the early stages. Some have no land yet, some have land but no buildings, and some are midway through construction. They often welcome new members because they need people, skills, and momentum. The big advantage is that you can help shape the culture, vision, and physical infrastructure from the ground up.

The tradeoff is higher risk. Early-stage communities sometimes lose steam, adapt their vision, or dissolve altogether. Leadership changes, funding gaps, zoning challenges, and personality mismatches are more common in this phase. That doesn't mean you shouldn't join—it just means to go slowly, ask good questions, and stay realistic.

Established communities, according to <u>ic.org</u>, are at least two years old with four or more adult members. These places have a track record. You can see what life actually looks like: the culture, the systems, the shared rhythms. Established communities offer more stability, clearer roles, and well-tested governance and membership processes. You won't be guessing what the place "might become" because it already is something.

The tradeoff is that openings are limited. Many established places are full and accept new members only when someone moves out. They may also be more structured, with less flexibility to change the culture or systems.

If you're unsure which category fits you, explore both. Visit a forming group (or attend a virtual meet up) to feel the energy of creation, then visit an established place to see how it all functions in real time. Most people find they have a natural preference once they experience both firsthand.

Tracking and Comparing Your Options

Community research gets messy fast. Names blend together. You forget who used consensus or sociocracy. One community had a swimming pool—wait, which one?

To help you keep this organized, I've created a **Communities Comparison Chart** you can download at **communityfinders.com/book1**. Make a copy of the spreadsheet and customize it.

Use it to compare communities on:

- Your Top 10 Wishlist
- Your Top 10 Avoid List
- Governance style
- Scale and size
- Culture
- Cost
- Housing availability
- Your intuition ("felt sense") after visiting

Use whatever scoring system feels natural: A/B/C, +/–, 1–10, or simple color coding.

Most important:

Leave room for intuition. If something feels right—or feels wrong—note it without needing a logical explanation.

Once you've filled in your chart, you'll start to see patterns. Some communities will rise to the top. Others will fall off the list.

This becomes your roadmap for the next stage: contacting communities and arranging visits.

CONTACTING COMMUNITIES

"Move at the speed of trust."

—ADRIENNE MAREE BROWN

You've found a few communities that look promising. You've read their websites, watched videos, maybe even spotted a photo and thought, *I could see myself there.*

Now comes the next step: reaching out.

And suddenly, it feels personal.

What do you say? How much should you share? What if they don't respond?

Many hopeful community seekers freeze at this stage. You're not alone. In my years of matchmaking and consulting, I've seen that the hardest part isn't finding communities—it's making that first connection with confidence and clarity.

This chapter will help you get a response and start the relationship on the right foot.

Before You Hit Send

First, understand what you're stepping into.

Most communities don't have paid staff answering inquiries. Messages usually land with a resident volunteer who's juggling their own life and a very full inbox. If you ever write to my community, that volunteer will be *me*—the person writing this book, running a couple of businesses, and still trying to reply gracefully to your query about visiting us next week!

If you never hear back, it probably isn't personal. It may simply mean the timing or the contact channel wasn't right. It's also possible the person reading your message didn't feel you were a fit. A response would have been courteous, of course, but sometimes it just doesn't come.

That said, there's a lot you can do to make your outreach stand out for all the right reasons.

1 · Keep It Short and Clear

Think "friendly postcard," not life story.

Your initial message should fit in one short paragraph. State who you are, why you're reaching out, and what you're asking for.

Something as simple as:

> **Subject:** Visiting Purrmaculture Community
> Hello Purrmaculture Team,
> I'm exploring intentional communities and was excited to learn about your focus on cats in permaculture and community gardens. I'd love to learn whether you're currently open to visitors or short-term stays.
> You can learn more about me on my social media page [link] or

in my community resume attached.
Warmly,
[Your Name]

That's it. Simple, respectful, human.

You can always share more later.

2 · Include a Way to Learn More About You

Communities appreciate concise emails, but they also need enough information to know who you are. This is a perfect moment to use the Community Resume you created earlier in the book.

Instead of writing a long personal history in your first message, include a link or attachment of your Community Resume. It gives a clear, grounded snapshot of who you are, what you value, and what you hope to contribute, without overwhelming the person reading your email.

If you already have an online presence—a simple website or social media page—you can add that too. And if you prefer to keep things private, a brief paragraph about your interests, skills, and why you're exploring community is enough.

3 · Do Your Research First

Nothing kills a first impression faster than asking questions already answered on their website.

Before reaching out, read what's publicly available about their mission, programs, and visiting options. Then, mention something specific that shows you've paid attention. For example:

> "I saw on your website that you hold open volunteer days on weekends. Are those still happening this season?"

This small detail signals that you value their time and culture. It's also a first act of reciprocity, showing respect before you even meet.

4 · Ask for One Clear Thing

Decide what you're asking before you write. Do you want to visit? Volunteer? Attend an event? Schedule a call?

Keep the request specific and realistic for a first contact. For example:

> "Would it be possible to visit for a day or join your next tour?"
> "Are you currently open to new members?"

Put your question on its own line for easy reading.

5 · Time Your Message Wisely

Reach out well ahead of when you'd like to visit. Ideally two to four months before longer trips, and at least a few weeks for local visits. Many communities need time to coordinate.

If you don't hear back within a week or two, it's okay to follow up with another email. If you still hear crickets, try a different method (for example, call or message through social media). After that, move on graciously.

Silence doesn't mean rejection. It often means the group is simply busy or in transition.

6 · Warm the Connection

Whenever possible, don't make your first contact completely cold. See if the community offers online events, volunteer opportunities, or public tours you can join beforehand. Mention a shared point of connection. "I attended your virtual open house" or "I heard about you through the FIC directory." This helps you feel like less of a stranger.

If you have mutual acquaintances, mention them respectfully and briefly. Shared context helps your message rise to the top of a full inbox.

7 · Treat It Like the Beginning of a Relationship

Reaching out to a community is less like sending an application and more like asking for a first conversation. Be kind, authentic, and patient. These are real people living real lives, not an organization built to process visitors.

You're initiating what could become a long-term relationship. First impressions matter, but so do humility and humor. Communities appreciate curiosity and respect far more than polished perfection.

The community I found isn't accepting members right now. Should I still reach out?

Short answer, yes.

Even if a community lists "no openings," it's still worth introducing yourself. Many communities have unadvertised opportunities—a room turning over, a member preparing to move, a sublet, or a trial period coming up that hasn't been posted yet. And if nothing is available, get on their mailing list or waiting list.

As intentional community becomes more popular (great for the movement, a little frustrating for seekers), many established places stay full. Openings often happen only when someone moves out or when new housing is created. Most communities share these opportunities with their email list first, and they may never be published publicly.

So don't skip a community just because it's full today. Stay connected. Introduce yourself. Let them know you're genuinely interested. You never know what tomorrow may bring.

The community never responded!

Don't take it personally. It's common for seekers to send several inquiries before getting a solid lead. Keep your message template handy and try again with another community. Each outreach teaches you something about tone, timing, and clarity.

Remember, there are always more communities in the sea.

A Simple Template

> **Subject:** Visiting [Name of Community]
> Hello [Name or Community Team],
> I'm exploring intentional communities and was excited to learn about your focus on [specific value, activity, or program].
> I'd love to find out whether you're currently open to visitors or short-term stays, and what the best next step might be.

I found your community through [source—directory, friend, online event].
You can learn more about me at [link to site or resume].
Looking forward to hearing from you,
[Your Name]

Think of every message as a seed. Some will land on rocky ground and never sprout. Others will grow and blossom in ways you never expected.

The best thing you can bring to this process is not the perfect email, but a spirit of curiosity and respect.

In the next chapter, we'll explore what happens *after* you make contact—how to plan, prepare for, and make the most of your first community visit.

VISITING COMMUNITIES

> "The best way to learn about yourself, and about the communities themselves, is to visit. In that context you can experiment with balancing work involvement with social involvement, and experience just how easy (or not!) it is for you to adapt to a new culture."
> —Geoph Kozeny, the Peripatetic Communitarian

If you've never visited an intentional community before, the idea can be both exciting and a little scary. What will the people be like? How comfortable will you feel there? Will you have to drink the Kool-Aid?!

Read on for advice on your first community visit.

Your Very First Community Visit

Your first community visit could be life-changing. You may be exposed to a different culture, new ideas, and inspiring people that open up whole worlds, much like traveling to a foreign country. Or your visit may be uninspiring or even negative.

Regardless of the experience, you will learn from it. At the very least, you'll discover what you like and don't like in a community, which is useful information when seeking a place to call home.

The guidance below will help you prepare. We'll cover planning your visit and what to pack, how to get the most from the experience, and how to leave a positive impression as a guest. This chapter is most suitable for overnight visits, but you'll also find helpful tips for day trips. It's especially designed for people who are new to intentional communities or considering membership.

If you're still deciding which communities to reach out to, review the earlier chapters on **Creating Your Community Wishlist**, **Types of People Drawn to Community**, and **Contacting Communities**. Your **Community Resume** can also help you introduce yourself with clarity.

Planning Your First Visit

There are multiple ways to visit, depending on distance, your availability, and the community's capacity. Be realistic about time off work, budget, and logistics. Start planning in advance.

Popular visit formats:

- **Day trip.** Best for nearby communities or casual visits. Often includes a tour, a community meal, or an open house.
- **Overnight stay.** Better than a single day for experiencing rhythm and culture.
- **Extended visit.** Several days to weeks or months if you're ready to go deeper; requires more advance planning.
- **Multiple return visits.** Ideal when transitioning slowly and wanting to deepen over time.

- **Multi-community trip.** The classic communities tour. You can do this solo or join a guided group tour with Ecovillage Tours at **ecovillagetours.com**.

A local day visit requires less planning than cross-country or international travel. For a larger trip or multi-stop tour, plan months ahead. Nearby day visits can be scheduled more spontaneously.

How to Start Planning Your Visit

Never ever just show up at a community!

Always confirm your welcome beforehand. You're visiting people's homes. Offer the same courtesy you would when visiting a new friend. Be respectful and communicate clearly from first contact to farewell.

- Make sure the community is open to visitors and secure permission well before arrival.
- Revisit **How to Contact a Community** for outreach guidance and a short email template.
- Some communities aren't open to visitors at all, or only on certain days or seasons. Others require joining a program—group tour, open house, retreat, or volunteer week.
- Before visiting, read as much as you can: the community's directory listing, website, or social media. Doing your research sets realistic expectations and helps the community trust that you'll be a considerate guest.

Get Clarity on Your Expectations

Clarity before you go helps you interpret the experience afterward.

- What are your goals for visiting? What do you hope to learn? Are you exploring membership, gathering ideas for a future project, or simply curious?
- Who do you hope to meet: founders, the membership coordinator, newer residents, other visitors?
- What activities interest you: meals, garden work, a meeting, a tour?

Culture matters. The more a community's culture differs from your normal life, the more intense your visit may feel. Groups set up for many guests can feel like a gentle "vacation." Projects on the experimental edge may feel more like a reality shift.

If the culture looks more radical, check in with yourself: are you open to new perspectives? Do you have time and support afterward to process a big experience? Consider planning a quiet day or two after the visit for reflection.

How Long to Stay

Generally, the longer you stay, the more you learn. Even a single overnight offers far more insight than a day visit. Many communities that host visitors provide basic overnight accommodations, at least a place to pitch a tent in season. Or they can recommend nearby lodging if none is available onsite.

That said, don't plan an overly long first visit. Better to come for a shorter stay and return if it feels like a fit. If you do sign up for a longer program (say several weeks or months), learn as much as you can beforehand. Talk by phone. Ask about expectations for long-term guests and how to end the experience early if needed.

Road Tripping to Multiple Communities

Pack up the van…it's time for a communities tour!

Journeying to multiple intentional communities during one or more extended trips can be the experience of a lifetime. You'll join the long tradition of travelers who hop from community to community, sharing stories, gathering wisdom, and gaining perspective as they go.

Below are some practical steps and considerations to help you make the most of your trip.

Decide on Your Mode of Transport

Many people on extended communities tours bring their home with them: a van (think #vanlife), an Airstream, a tiny house on wheels, a converted vegetable-oil school bus, a car with a rooftop tent, or even a bicycle set up for long-distance camping. In fact, there is a wonderful documentary about a couple who did a cross-country communities tour by bicycle, *Within Reach* (2012). You'll find endless inspiration for creative ways to design your own road-trip adventure by searching online.

Rural intentional communities often appreciate visitors who arrive with their own accommodations and simply need a place to park. Urban communities, on the other hand, can be tricky when it comes to parking a large camper.

That said, you do **not** need a mobile home to do a communities tour. Flying, taking the train, or riding the bus can sometimes be easier and more affordable.

Think through the distances you want to cover, the geography you'll be moving through, and what kind of travel best supports your comfort, budget, and style.

Plan Your Route

Some people cluster communities by region and make multiple smaller trips. For example, a Southeast US tour one year and a Central Europe tour the next. Others choose a single cross-country journey and visit everything along the way.

Older, well-established communities often become hubs, with newer forming communities springing up around them. This can be due to the pioneering work of the original community, a strong alternative culture in the area, or practical reasons like affordable land or permissive zoning.

So when visiting a well-known place like Dancing Rabbit in Missouri or Twin Oaks in Virginia, check what other communities are nearby. It's often easy to visit several in one trip.

Always take advantage of communities along your route. Even if a place doesn't seem like your future home, visiting increases your experience, perspective, and clarity. Every visit teaches you something—sometimes what you want, sometimes what you don't.

Between community stays, expect to rely on hotels, Airbnbs, or campgrounds. Communities may be far apart or have limited availability. And sometimes you'll simply need a night off. Solo time between visits is wonderful for reflection and rest before meeting a whole new group of people.

Arranging Your Stay

Once you've reached out and received the green light to visit, it's time to finalize details.

Below is a list of questions you *may* ask in advance. You don't need to send the full list—just the pieces that apply to you and aren't already clarified on the website. If email feels slow, get on the phone.

Be sure to consider the needs of everyone in your party, especially children or anyone with special requirements.

Questions to Ask Before You Visit

- Who will greet me or show me around when I arrive?
- Are there any specific norms or practices I should know?
- Will I be expected to join any meetings or work periods?
- What should I bring? Will meals be provided?
- Is there a preferred diet for shared meals?
- May I use the kitchen or fridge?
- How do visitors cover expenses, and what is the amount?
- Anything else I should know?

Additional Questions Depending on Your Circumstances

- Any instructions for arriving with my vehicle?
- Parking guidelines?
- Can I bring my dog or other pet?
- Can I bring my children (and what ages)?
- Can I bring a group, and how many?

Expect to be met by someone when you arrive. Confirm their name and contact info so you can reach them if plans shift.

Once arrangements are made…time to pack.

Packing List for YourCommunity Visit

Below is a list of items you may want to bring in addition to your normal clothes and traveling needs. The dress code in most intentional living communities is comfortable and casual.

Considering bringing:

- **A guest gift to smaller communities.** Think of something inexpensive yet meaningful that fits in your luggage. This could be a special food item that comes from your region (garden seeds, cheese, a sweet, cooking oil, etc.) or something you've made (decoration for their common room, piece of art, soap, candle, etc.)
- **A notebook and camera.** Great for jotting down facts while on a tour and reflections during the experience. Ask before taking photos.
- **Your musical instrument.** Or a song, story, or game to share after dinner or around the fire.
- **Camping gear or work gloves/boots.** Depending on the visit and how likely you are to be spending time outdoors.
- **Positivity and a friendly smile.**

Staying Safe During Your Visit

With good research and communication, unsafe situations are rare—but preparation matters.

Do Your Research

Look for up-to-date information, photos, visitor reviews, or references from others who have been there. If the group seems overly idealistic or vague, ask clarifying questions.

Have an Exit Strategy

Make sure you have independent transportation or a clear plan for leaving if needed.

Tell Someone Where You're Going

Leave your itinerary with a friend or family member and check in regularly.

Warning Signs May Include:

- Pressure to contribute financially without clear agreements
- Pressure to participate in anything beyond your comfort
- Power imbalances (for example, a founder pursuing relationships with new or younger members)

If anything feels unsafe, leave immediately and seek help.

Making the Most of Your Visit

You've arrived, met your hosts, settled in, and the real experience begins.

Below are some questions you can ask the person showing you around. Ideally you can speak to more residents than just your host. Listen for both what is said and what is lived.

Questions to Ask During Your Visit

- How did you come to be part of this community?
- How has living here contributed to your personal growth or happiness?
- What are the community's big dreams and goals? Core values?
- What are some difficult issues the community has had to deal with recently?
- How do you handle interpersonal conflicts?
- How has the community changed over the years? Increased or decreased in diversity?
- How are decisions made?
- Who owns the land and buildings (and pays for maintenance)?
- How do people join the community? What are the costs to join?
- Why do members tend to leave the community?

Consider the questions above as prompts for conversation, not a tally of answers you need to reach.

As Julie Pennington reminds us in a *Communities* magazine article (in the Spring 2004 issue), ask if it is okay to ask! "Before dumping a mass of questions on someone, ask if it is a convenient time to ask about the community. Don't be offended if the honest answer is 'No.' What for you is a vacation spot is really someone's home, and members have responsibilities and lives of their own that they have to address."

Being a Welcomed Guest

Below is some advice for how you can be remembered as a great guest:

- **Follow the rules and agreements.** Pay attention to signs and notices posted in rooms (especially the kitchen) or along pathways. You don't know why certain things were agreed to; just go along.
- **Consider the whole property as someone's private property.** Stick to designated walking areas, take off your shoes when entering buildings if you notice that's the custom, give folks their space.
- **Learn how systems work before using them.** Especially for washing up, heating, using tools, laundry, etc.
- **Be aware of your own energy and how it affects others.** Be authentic yet respectful.
- **Don't take it personally if someone is grumpy or doesn't greet you.** Everyone has an off-day and you are a stranger wandering around their home.
- **Ask before taking photos.** Remember that you are visiting someone's home and not a tourist destination.
- **Offer to clean dishes and help with chores.** Best way to make a positive impression.
- Send a thank you note afterwards!

If you hope to become a member someday, ask yourself: *How will these people remember me?* Do what you can to have them remember you well.

Attending Community Meetings

Being welcomed to join a community meeting is a great opportunity and should be taken advantage of. Don't assume you will be invited, but if it happens, do go!

This is a fantastic way to get an insider's view of the community dynamics. You'll get to pick up on the culture of the residents by how they speak to one another, how they listen, and how quickly they are able to move through the agenda and make decisions.

Tips:

- Ask where to sit.
- Ask how long the meeting will run.
- Sit quietly unless invited to speak.
- If you have genuinely helpful information relevant to the topic, politely ask if you may share.
- Keep anything discussed confidential.

Managing Expectations

First-time visitors often arrive with a lot of idealism. It's natural. You've been dreaming about community, maybe for years, and now you're finally getting to walk the land and meet the people.

But high expectations can set you up for disappointment if you imagine life in community to look like a constant festival of harmony, productivity, and human connection.

For example, when visiting an ecovillage, some guests expect the community to grow all their own food and run entirely on renewable energy. Ecovillages are living models for the future world, after all!

In reality, most residents are simply doing their best to manage their families, work, and finances—just like anyone else. And when glossy websites or profiles paint a picture that is more aspirational than factual, the gap between expectation and lived reality can feel jarring.

Another common expectation is emotional: people imagine a community to be warm, vibrant, and instantly welcoming, with residents bursting into song or circling up around the fire the moment you arrive. Sometimes that *does* happen. More often, you've just shown up on a Tuesday afternoon between chores, work shifts, and getting the kids to soccer.

Keep in mind that every community goes through waves of activity and quiet. If things felt slow or subdued during your visit, it may simply have been an off-week—or the community may thrive in ways that aren't immediately visible to a newcomer. There is often much more happening beneath the surface than you're able to perceive in a short stay.

And if you don't instantly feel like you've met your new best friends, that's normal. Deep belonging takes time. Most communities aren't equipped to offer instant emotional intimacy to guests. They're not therapy centers, and expecting them to meet unspoken relational needs can leave you feeling let down.

It helps to hold your idealism lightly. Remember: *most people who try to start communities never succeed.* The fact that the places you're visiting exist at all is already a small miracle. Approach them with gratitude, curiosity, and humility.

Debriefing Your Visit Experience

After your visit:

- Review your notes.
- Consider how you *felt*—energized, overwhelmed, neutral?
- Cross-check your experience with your Community Wishlist.
- Notice surprises, disappointments, and delights.

If something didn't go well, ask what can be learned—not only about the community, but about yourself.

Every visit teaches you something.

Why Join an Ecovillage Tour to Visit Communities

Over the years of coaching, I've noticed the same pattern again and again. People get curious about community living, they research endlessly, they dream big…and then they get stuck at the very same bottleneck: actually *visiting* communities.

Travel logistics are overwhelming. They don't know where to go first, how to make contact, or how to arrange several visits efficiently. Many are afraid of "bothering" communities or worried about making a misstep. Others simply felt too alone in the process.

I created Ecovillage Tours to remove that barrier.

Our trips are designed for people who are curious about community life and want to experience it firsthand in a supportive, structured way. Instead of spending weeks coordinating logistics, participants visit a range of communities in a single journey, guided by people who know the terrain, the culture, and the questions to ask.

Each tour becomes a kind of temporary village in itself—a traveling community of seekers who learn from one another, share reflections, and often continue supporting each other long after the trip ends. Along the way, participants receive real guidance on their path, especially from the local guides we partner with, who are themselves experts in the field,

Many past travelers have gone on to join the very communities they visited. Others gained the insight, clarity, or confidence they needed to take the next step in their personal community journey.

Visiting communities should not be the hardest part of finding home. My hope is that these tours make the path easier, more joyful, and far more connected.

Come join a tour in destinations worldwide at **ecovillagetours.com**.

We have regular trips throughout the United States, Europe, Central America, and Asia. Most trips are one to two weeks in length. We visit ecovillages as well as many other forms of intentional community living.

Now that you've begun to experience real communities up close, the next step is learning how to more deeply evaluate what you saw.

In the following chapter, we'll look more closely at how to recognize signs of health, signs of distress, and how to determine whether a community is truly a good fit for you—before you take any big steps toward joining.

VETTING COMMUNITIES

> "A healthy brain is defined by having many connections between its cells, just as a healthy community is defined by having many connections between its people."
>
> —Jill Bolte Taylor

To *vet* a community means thoroughly evaluating its suitability before committing to join.

Most people hope to find a community that is already functioning well, though some feel drawn to help heal a struggling one.

I like to think of *community health* much the way I think about *ecosystem health*. In the natural world, well-being is often measured by the quality *and* quantity of exchange among species. The same is true for human communities. How much interaction is happening between members, and what is the quality of those interactions?

A community with lots of connection is said to have strong "community glue." There are many ways that glue gets made: shared projects, regular meetings, potlucks, work parties, celebrations, and the small daily exchanges that weave people together.

It's often said that a healthy community can be measured by how often meals are shared. I'd say that's true—to a point. One rather dysfunctional community I knew had breakfast, lunch, and dinner together every day. Let's just say the salt was not always passed! **Quality** matters just as much as frequency.

Early in their search, people often ask me, "Are there any communities that have it all figured out?" What they're usually hoping for is longevity, harmony, and solid structure. Sensible enough. No one wants drama, disorganization, or spiritual bypassing.

But here's the truth: if you're looking for a place that has never had conflict and will remain unchanged forever, you are chasing a mirage. Communities are living systems. They cycle. They grow and shed. Some even *end well*. Perpetuity is not the point. Connection is.

This chapter will help you learn how to read what you're seeing: the signs of health, the subtle red flags, the founder factor, and the questions that turn "good vibes" into grounded understanding.

The Red Flag That Sounds Reassuring

"We've never had any problems."

If a group claims to have no conflict, don't feel relieved. Feel curious. Conflict is natural. What matters is how a group talks about it and what they do when it appears.

Healthy communities don't avoid tension. They acknowledge difficulty, use systems to work through it, and learn. If issues are denied or minimized, communication and psychological safety may be weak.

Related myth: Age equals success. Longevity can be good, but it isn't everything. Some long-running groups persist because they resist change. Others dissolve gracefully when the energy shifts. A community that chooses to end well can be healthier than one that clings.

What Healthy Actually Looks Like

When you visit, look for **process**, not polish.

- **Open communication.** People can name hard topics without freezing the room.
- **Conflict systems that are used.** Clear steps for raising concerns, getting facilitation, and making repair. We'll go deeper in the **When Conflict Happens** chapter.
- **Cultural evolution.** Stories about "how we used to do it" and what changed.
- **Multiple voices.** You hear different perspectives, not a single spokesperson.
- **Whole stories.** Members share joys and challenges: "It's been a tough season, and here's how we're working it."
- **Clues of connection.** Shared projects, rituals, celebrations, mutual aid.

I often say the best way to assess health is to observe how a community moves through difficulty. Are people growing together or growing apart?

The Founder Factor: Power, Ownership, and the Shift to "We"

Many newer communities begin with a strong founder. That's not automatically a problem; someone has to start the fire. What happens next is crucial.

Warning signs in founder-led groups:

- Founder owns the land with no credible plan to share ownership or leadership.

- "We tried, but no one was a good fit."
- Decisions are "shared" in name only.
- No written pathway for joining, contributing, or leaving.

It's a classic chicken-and-egg. People hesitate to invest where power isn't truly shared; founders hesitate to share with people who haven't invested. This gap can be bridged by transparency and agreements.

Questions to ask in early-stage or founder-led communities:

- What is the ownership structure now, and what is the timeline to diversify it?
- How are decisions made today, and how will that evolve?
- What are the steps to join, contribute, and exit? What do I keep if I leave?
- Which agreements are written and enforceable?

Trust your sense of relationship. Then ask for it in writing.

Due Diligence: Documents Worth Reading

As you inch closer towards membership, ask to see:

- **Membership pathway.** Steps, timelines, evaluations, fees, and trial periods.
- **Governance.** Bylaws, consent/consensus policy, role descriptions, selection processes, meeting cadence.
- **Land and ownership.** Deeds, leases, homeowners association (HOA)/condo docs, land trust or co-op agreements, resale or right-of-first-refusal policies.
- **Finance.** Dues, budgets, reserves, transparency practices, work-trade expectations.

- **Community agreements.** Conduct, conflict, care, safety, pets, children, quiet hours, guests, labor.
- **Exit and conflict procedures.** How people leave. How harms are addressed. What appeal or review exists.

You do not need a law degree. You need the willingness to ask, "Where is this written?" and "How does this work in practice?"

A newer community may not have all of these documents created yet, but an established community most certainly will. Remember to trust, but verify.

When You're Close to a Yes

Before a big commitment:

- Do a second visit in a different season or weekday rhythm.
- Experience at least one governance meeting and one shared work block.
- Review documents with a family member, friend, or professional who can ask tough questions.
- Consider the commute, schooling, healthcare, or other critical logistics.
- Clarify trial periods, deposits, refunds, and exit paths in writing.

If something feels off and you can't name it, you don't have enough information yet.

If You Spot a Red Flag or Experience a Community in Distress

Name the concern respectfully and see how the group responds. A healthy community can hear feedback and offer clarity. If you are pressured, minimized, or shamed for asking basic questions, that is your signal.

There is no perfect community. There are healthy ones, and there are healthy choices you can make while you search. Stay curious. Trust your gut, then test your gut with observation.

It's also good to remember that communities can dip into periods of distress.

My own community went through this a few years back when our founder was leaving. Had you visited us then, you would have thought we were a hot mess, and honestly we were. But now, some time later, the dust has settled, new families have moved in, and by my own assessment things are quite healthy.

Perspective matters too. I once had a client write to tell me how much she loved her visit to a community I had recommended. Then, just a week later, someone else wrote with a nightmare story from visiting the very same place, possibly even in the same week. What I think happened is that the second person arrived with certain assumptions, like expecting all meals to be provided and expecting people to go out of their way to spend time with her.

It's a good reminder of Anaïs Nin's words: "We don't see things as they are, we see them as we are."

Assuming everything checks out, and you think you're onto a community that's a great fit, it's time for the big moment: deciding to say yes! The next chapter will help you get to yes (or no) with confidence and clarity.

STEPPING INTO MEMBERSHIP

> "My humanity is bound up in yours, for we can only be human together."
>
> —Desmond Tutu

Finding a community that feels right is one of the most exciting stages of this entire process.

It is also where things become more real. Visiting is one thing. Imagining is another. But choosing a community to join is an intimate decision, a bit like choosing who to build a life with. It requires clarity, honesty, and a willingness to step into relationship.

In mainstream housing, you pick a house and hope the neighbors are decent. In intentional communities, the script is reversed. You meet the people first and only then decide whether you want to make a home among them.

Some people arrive at this point ready to leap. Others need time, reflection, and many conversations. There is no right way to make this choice. There is only your way.

This chapter will guide you through how to decide on a community to join and how to navigate the membership process once you are ready.

Understanding the Membership Process

Once you find a community that resonates with you, your first step is to understand how people actually join. Every intentional community has its own membership pathway. Some are very structured with clear stages. Others are more informal and fluid. Your job is to learn the steps and expectations so that you can participate with confidence.

Reach out and ask about their process. Communities usually outline the basics on their website, but it is always worth confirming. They may have an application, interviews, a trial stay, or a provisional membership period. They may have shared work requirements or a particular rhythm of participation. They may also have a timeline that stretches over months.

It is a two-way street. You are learning how the community gets to know new people and how new people get to know the community. You are evaluating them and they are evaluating you.

In *Finding Community* by Diana Leafe Christian, there's a great quote from Irwin Wolfe Zucker:

"If your community front door is difficult to enter, healthy people will strive to get in."

So be glad when a community has a stringent membership process. It means they're taking great care with whom they welcome, all in service of preserving the health of their community. The world is full of people who are yearning for community yet not quite ready to live in one. Communities must screen for emotional maturity, conscious communication, and a willingness to contribute.

A Helpful Metaphor: Courtship to Commitment

Although processes vary, many communities follow a similar arc. It can be useful to imagine it like the stages of developing a relationship with a life partner.

Courtship:
This is the early stage where you visit, meet residents, participate in work parties, and get acquainted with the culture and agreements. You ask questions and they ask questions. Both sides feel out the fit.

Making a Move:
At a certain point, you express your intention to join. This may involve an application, interviews, references, financial conversations, or background checks. You begin to step forward more clearly.

Engagement:
Many communities have a provisional period. You live there or participate as an associate member, but you do not yet have all the rights or responsibilities of full membership. This period often lasts several months to a year. Some communities create trial periods that double as training programs, helping people learn the skills they expect from members. Others may recommend books, workshops, or trainings you can pursue on your own.

Marriage:
This is full membership. Depending on the community, it might mean purchasing a home, joining a cooperative, taking on governance responsibilities, or formally committing to shared values.

Your path may look different from this outline, but the theme is the same. Community membership unfolds slowly, through trust and transparency. Longer processes are often signs of maturity. They help ensure that both you and the community build a stable foundation.

Legal Realities of Choosing Members

Membership selection in intentional communities exists within a legal framework. In the US, any group that provides housing is subject to fair housing laws. These laws allow communities to screen for values alignment, communication skills, willingness to follow agreements, and the ability to meet participation expectations. What they cannot do is accept or reject people based on protected traits such as race, religion, sex, disability, family status, or national origin. Most countries have similar protections.

Different legal models do not change this. Cohousing HOAs, rental co-ops, nonprofit ecovillages, Private Membership Associations, religious-designated groups, and income-sharing communes all must follow fair housing rules when housing is involved. In practice, this means communities can evaluate whether someone is prepared to participate, uphold agreements, and live cooperatively, but not anything tied to protected categories.

What Membership Processes Actually Look Like

To give you a realistic sense of what membership processes look like in practice, here are examples from actual communities. I've simplified them a bit, but stayed accurate to how they typically operate.

Cohousing: Clear, Practical, and Often Quick

Cohousing communities tend to have the simplest and most predictable membership process. Because the model is based on homeownership, the main steps revolve around understanding the culture, getting to know residents, and navigating the practicalities of buying a home.

Most cohousing groups I have spoken with rely on what they often call "self-selection." They invite prospective residents to participate enough to decide for themselves whether the community is a fit.

Places like Pioneer Valley Cohousing or Durham Cohousing start with a public tour or orientation, often held monthly. If you're still interested, you meet with their membership team, share a meal with residents, attend one meeting, and review their documents. When a unit becomes available, you apply to join the HOA and purchase the home.

There is, however, a unique pressure in cohousing that does not show up as strongly in other models: resale tension. Outgoing homeowners may be eager to sell their homes quickly and recoup their investment. At the same time, the community often wants to ensure that incoming residents understand the commitments involved and have spent enough time getting to know people. Balancing the seller's timeline with the community's desire for thoughtful integration can create friction, especially when the housing market is moving fast.

Typical timeline:
About one to six months. Mostly dependent on housing availability.

Ecovillages: Slower, Relationship-Centered, and Culturally Deep

Ecovillages usually ask for more integration. Their structure as a community land trust, nonprofit, cooperative, or rental-based village allows for greater flexibility and creativity with membership. Communities like Dancing Rabbit or Earthaven usually require a visitor period—anything from a long weekend to an "Experience Week," followed by reviewing their agreements and meeting with their membership circle.

If there is mutual interest, you may enter a provisional membership phase (called "New Roots" at Earthaven) where you live on-site for several months with the support of a resident host or buddy. You join work parties, meetings, and daily rhythms before being voted in as a full member, which may take anywhere from one to two years.

Typical timeline:
Six months to two years, depending on how often you visit and how committed you are.

Income-Sharing Communities: Slow, Careful, and Highly Relational

Income-sharing communities have the longest and most selective processes. In places like Twin Oaks or Acorn Community in Virginia, the first step is a written application followed by a required visitor period (Twin Oaks requires three weeks). If the group sees potential, you move into a provisional membership period of six to twelve months. A full membership vote comes only after the community has lived, worked, and made decisions with you for some time.

Typical timeline:
One to three years from first contact to full membership.

Forming Communities: Flexible, Messy, and Full of Potential

Forming communities vary widely. Some begin with Zoom calls and interest groups; others invite people to camping weekends or shared work parties. You might help choose land, draft values, or test governance processes before anything is built. Only when land is secured do early members usually make a financial commitment and formalize membership.

Typical timeline:
Anywhere from six months to six years. Forming communities move at the speed of trust, alignment, and project management.

How to Decide

Once you have visited communities and reviewed their membership processes, the next step is choosing where to land. This is part practical decision and part inner listening.

Start by looking at what you gathered earlier. Return to your Community Comparison Chart, your notes, and your Community Wishlist. Notice which communities truly align with your non-negotiables and which fall short. A little objective review helps prevent wishful thinking or overlooking red flags.

Then shift into a different mode. Picture a normal day in each community, not a special event or a tour. How does your body feel there? Relaxed, energized, cramped, uncertain? Sometimes the clearest guidance shows up as a simple sense of "I can breathe here" or "Something feels off." Intuition tends to be quiet and steady. Fear tends to be urgent and tense. Learn to tell them apart.

If you feel pulled in two directions, revisit your notes and your body until something starts to feel clearer. If a community matches nearly everything but feels flat when you're there, trust that. If another misses a few wishlist items but lights you up inside, look closer. The right choice is often where logic and inner resonance meet.

At some point, you have to choose. Not with perfect certainty, but with enough clarity to take the next step. Joining a community is never about finding a flawless paradise. It is about choosing a place where you can grow, contribute, and imagine a real life for yourself.

Let your mind sort the facts.
Let your intuition feel the truth.
Then choose the place where both say yes.

A Note About Rejection

You may be turned down at some point in the membership process. It happens more often than people think. Communities sometimes say no for reasons that have nothing to do with your potential as a communitarian. They may be full, burned out, shifting direction, or simply unsure.

Even I was once turned down by a community, believe it or not! Looking back, I realize it would not have been the right move for me. On a whim, I applied to a community in California where I had visited a few times and had some friends. It would have been a huge life shift and not one I had fully thought through. I think the community sensed that. They ended up choosing someone local, an expectant mother who became a beautifully grounded addition to their circle.

It is reasonable to ask what might cause a prospective member to be declined. And it is okay to ask after you've been denied, not to challenge the decision but to learn from it for next time.

Decision Fatigue and Decision Clarity

Some people commit too quickly. Others get paralyzed by too many options. Both behaviors are understandable.

Ask yourself:

Have you visited enough communities to make a grounded comparison?
If not, visit more.

Have you visited so many that everything is a blur?
If so, slow down. Return to your Wishlist. Let yourself choose.

Are you hesitating out of fear?
Name the fear. Is it about the place, or about allowing yourself to belong?

Is your intuition nudging you?
Trust it. Intuition is not fantasy. It is the sum of your lived experience speaking through your body.

The right moment to commit often arrives with a quiet sense of readiness, not fireworks. Listen for that.

After You Join: The Natural Stages

Joining a community is a beginning, not an ending. After membership, most people pass through a few common stages which can again parallel the development of a married relationship.

The Honeymoon:
Everything feels magical. The potlucks, the conversations, the children playing, the shared projects. You cannot believe you waited so long to

find this.

The Honeymoon Ends:
Reality appears. Meetings feel too long. People give too much feedback. The shared spaces get messy. You wonder if you made a mistake.

Acceptance and Understanding:
With time, patience, and deeper relationship, you settle in. You understand the value of slowing down, listening well, and building trust. You begin to feel at home.

Leaving (sometimes):
People leave communities for many reasons: major life changes, unmet needs, burnout, or simply the natural seasons of life. Leaving is not failure. It is part of the life cycle of community.

Choosing a community is one of the most personal and meaningful decisions you will make. It is not only about land or houses or membership forms. It is about choosing the people with whom you will share your days, your work, your celebrations, and your challenges.

As you step into this choice, let your clarity, your courage, and your relationships guide you. And know that your presence will not just fit into a community. It will help shape it.

Next we'll go deeper into what it means to join a community (or build it) depending on your phase of life.

PART IV:

PRACTICAL CONSIDERATIONS

HOW MUCH DOES IT COST?

> "In a gift economy, the more you give,
> the richer you are."
> —Charles Eisenstein

By this point in your exploration, you may be wondering some practical questions, foremost:

How much will this actually cost?

Can I afford to live in one of these communities or not?

Too often people get excited about the idea of community living, start exploring directories, fall in love with photos of gardens and common houses, then feel their heart sink when they see the price tag.

Every week I hear from people who long for connection, sustainability, and shared purpose, but who have little or no money to put toward it. They feel like the very lifestyle that could support them is financially out of reach.

The truth is that there is no single answer. The cost of living in an intentional community can range from more expensive than conventional housing to dramatically more affordable, depending on where it is, how it is structured, and what kind of life you want to lead.

This chapter will help you understand why costs vary so widely, what kinds of models tend to be more affordable, and how to think creatively about your own path, even if your budget feels tight right now.

The Housing Crisis, and Why Communities Are Not Immune

We are living through a global housing crisis. Prices have risen faster than wages in many regions, rental markets are tight, and homeownership is out of reach for a growing number of people.

Intentional communities are not magically outside of this reality. Communities still need to buy land, build or renovate homes, pay for infrastructure, and maintain roads, roofs, and septic systems. They do this inside the same economic system everyone else lives in.

Sometimes people imagine that intentional communities ought to be free or nearly free, as if they exist on a different planet where money does not apply.

In practice, communities are doing their best to create something more cooperative in the middle of a very unequal capitalist economy. Some succeed at keeping costs low. Others, especially in high-value areas, end up as expensive as the surrounding housing market.

Cohousing projects near thriving cities, for instance, often look very similar financially to any other condominium or townhouse development in the area. That can feel discouraging if you are hoping community will be your "affordable housing solution."

At the same time, many communities are actively experimenting with more accessible models: shared ownership, cooperatives, income sharing, land trusts, and resident-owned neighborhoods. These experiments matter, because they point toward what could be possible on a larger scale.

One important note here:
If you or someone you love is in an immediate housing crisis, intentional communities are rarely a quick fix. Most have careful membership processes that take months or even years, and they may not be equipped for emergency shelter. If you are in urgent need of housing, please reach out locally for crisis support first, then consider intentional communities as a longer-term path once you have some stability.

"It Depends": Geography and Model Matter

Just as in mainstream housing, geography makes a huge difference. A three-bedroom home in rural Missouri will not cost the same as a similar home outside Seattle or Boston. The same is true in community.

Here are a few real-world examples that show the range:

- At Rooted Northwest, a forming cohousing community outside Seattle, home prices start around eight hundred thousand dollars. This reflects the very high real estate costs in the Pacific Northwest.
- At Earthaven Ecovillage in rural North Carolina, some residents rent simple apartments or cabins for a few hundred dollars per month. These costs can be further reduced through work exchange, growing food, or shared infrastructure.
- At Twin Oaks Community, an income-sharing community in Virginia, people can join with very little money. Members contribute labor to community businesses and receive housing, food, healthcare access, and a monthly stipend in return.
- At Beacon Hill Friends House in Boston, residents rent private rooms in a large shared home organized as a nonprofit. For an urban environment, this can be a relatively affordable way to live with others in the city center.

Rural ecovillages, community land trusts, and rural cooperatives often fall on the more affordable side. Urban cohousing, coliving, and ownership-based communities in expensive cities will usually be higher cost.

Exploring communities outside of major metropolitan zones, or even outside your current country, can dramatically expand the range of financially realistic options.

Different Community Models, Different Money Systems

Each type of intentional community tends to use a different financial structure. Understanding these differences will help you focus your search where it makes the most sense.

Cohousing

Cohousing communities are usually based on private homeownership combined with shared common spaces. You purchase a home or unit and then pay monthly dues to a homeowners association or similar body for shared expenses.

If you cannot qualify for a mortgage, or you do not have cash for a down payment, cohousing may be challenging at first. Some cohousing groups, however, work hard to include more affordable or rental options inside their projects. Burlington Cohousing in Vermont, for example, is part of a Community Land Trust, which helps to subsidize a portion of the units so they are within reach for lower and middle income residents.

Housing co-ops and group houses

Co-ops and collectives are often based on shared ownership or rental. You might buy a share in a cooperative that owns the building, or you might join a group house where everyone shares rent and utilities. Monthly costs tend to be lower than market-rate apartments in the same city, although this varies.

Income-sharing communities and communes
Income-sharing communities like East Wind or Acorn pool member income and labor. The community covers essential needs, such as housing, food, and basic healthcare access. There is usually no buy-in cost, but there is a clear expectation of work inside the community businesses and household systems.

These communities can be very affordable in cash terms, but they ask a lot in terms of participation and cultural fit. They also represent only a small percentage of intentional communities overall. Most communities have separate finances and simply share some expenses, rather than fully pooling income.

Ecovillages
Ecovillages range widely, from off-grid projects in the countryside to small villages with modern homes and fiber internet. Some have ownership models where you buy a lease or small lot. Others offer rentals, work exchange, or the option to build or park a tiny house. Costs also range widely. Some ecovillages are quite expensive, others are among the most affordable options available.

Community Land Trusts (CLTs)
CLTs are nonprofit entities that own land for the long term and keep it permanently out of speculative real estate markets. Residents typically buy or lease homes on that land under long-term agreements, such as 99-year leases.

Because the land itself is not bought and sold like a normal asset, entry costs can be significantly lower. The tradeoff is that resale prices are often capped, so you may not see the same equity growth as in a conventional home. This invites deep questions about how we relate to wealth, legacy, and housing as an investment.

Coliving communities
Coliving spaces, especially in cities, are usually commercial enterprises that rent furnished rooms or micro-units in a building with shared amenities. They can be more affordable than renting a full apartment alone and offer built-in social life, although most are not designed for families and may not include shared ownership or governance.

Resident-Owned Communities (ROCs) and manufactured home co-ops
Some of the most affordable community models in North America are resident-owned manufactured home communities. In these neighborhoods, residents have collectively bought the land under their homes and run it as a cooperative. ROC USA has helped hundreds of such communities make this transition from private ownership to resident ownership.

Monthly lot fees can be relatively low compared to market rents, and residents have stable control over their land. While these places may not always use the label "intentional community," the cooperative structure and shared decision-making place them firmly inside the broader movement.

How Communities Make Housing More Affordable

Alongside individual affordability, there is a larger story: intentional communities experimenting with more just and sustainable housing on purpose. Here are some of the key strategies that I see communities using.

Reducing building costs
Some communities lower costs by using natural building techniques like strawbale, cob, or light-earth construction. When people pool skills, tools, and labor, they can build simple, beautiful homes at a fraction of conventional costs.

Other communities partner with innovative prefab builders. Geoship, for example, is developing bio-ceramic geodesic homes that are designed to be both climate resilient and relatively affordable. Models like this can pair well with communities that have land, volunteers, and a shared vision, but limited access to conventional capital.

Redefining equity and ownership
Rather than tying wealth solely to rising property values, some communities adopt models that balance access and equity. Community Land Trusts cap resale values to keep homes affordable for the next generation. Some co-ops allow shares to appreciate slowly, but not to speculative levels.

These models invite residents to ask: "How much is enough, and what do I want to pass on? Maximum personal gain, or housing security for those who come after me?" There is no single right answer, but intentional communities are where these questions are being worked out in real time.

Transforming the HOA model
In many conventional neighborhoods, the homeowners association is something people complain about. Rules are set from the top, enforcement is punitive, and residents feel more regulated than empowered.

In intentional communities, the same legal structure can function very differently. Residents themselves typically design the bylaws, decide how to spend shared funds, and use cooperative decision-making practices. In this way, the HOA or condo association becomes a tool for self-governance, rather than an outside authority.

Reducing dependence on landlords
Where renting is involved, communities often aim to reduce the power imbalance between landlord and tenant. Sometimes the "landlord" is actually the cooperative or nonprofit that residents themselves manage. Sometimes a single owner lives on site and sees renting as a long-term partnership with neighbors, not a profit-maximizing enterprise.

In manufactured home parks that flip to resident ownership, for example, residents are no longer at the mercy of sudden lot rent hikes or park sales. Instead, they collectively decide about improvements, rents, and maintenance.

Creative funding and subsidies
Affordable communities rarely appear out of nowhere. They are usually built through a mix of creativity and persistence. Some of the approaches I see include:

- Government grants or subsidies for low-income units
- Nonprofits raising funds specifically for affordable homes
- Low-interest loans from aligned individuals or foundations
- Rent-to-own agreements that ease the path into ownership
- Adding accessory dwelling units (ADUs) to create smaller, lower-cost homes
- Community-owned businesses that generate income for shared infrastructure
- Setting aside a percentage of homes for low-income residents

None of these solutions is perfect on its own. Together, they point toward a housing ecosystem that is more cooperative and resilient.

Pairing needs and gifts
Some of the most inspiring models of affordable community life arise when groups pair complementary needs.

Treehouse Communities, for instance, are intergenerational neighborhoods that support families raising children from the foster care system while giving elders a way to live with purpose and connection. Elders gain meaning and community, while children gain stability and support.

Other programs match seniors with younger housemates, or veterans with volunteers in community-like villages. Bastion in New Orleans is one example, where injured veterans and their families live alongside military and civilian volunteers in a supportive neighborhood.

These models show that affordability is not just about lowering rent. It is about designing communities that share care, responsibility, and resilience.

Building a culture of sharing

Finally, at the heart of affordable intentional communities is a simple cultural shift: people share more.

Sometimes sharing is very extensive: communal meals, shared work, and pooled incomes. More often, it looks like a return to village life. People borrow tools instead of each household buying its own. They share childcare. They trade rides, skills, and food.

As more of life comes into the realm of "ours" rather than "mine," many costs naturally go down. You may not need your own guest room if there are shared guest spaces. You may not need your own full workshop if the community has one. You may buy fewer appliances, books, or toys when they can be shared.

Some communities embrace elements of a gift economy, where shared reciprocity—rather than strict accounting—guides how people exchange support.

For example, in my community, we try not to stress over who contributes what to the garden or how many veggies each person takes. Our aim is simply to grow an overabundance so there's always enough to share. It's amazing how bringing a spirit of abundance, rather than scarcity, into a system can make everything flow more easily for everyone.

Sharing is not just about saving money. It is also about creating a daily fabric of generosity, reciprocity, and belonging.

Rethinking What "Home" Means

When people ask, "How much does it cost to live in an intentional community," they are often picturing a very specific thing: a private house, similar to what they have now, but located inside a community. That certainly exists. It is not the only option.

Living in community often means living smaller privately and larger collectively. You might move from a three-bedroom house into a one-bedroom unit with access to guest rooms, gardens, play spaces, common rooms, a workshop, and shared vehicles.

Many people find this shift liberating. They discover that what really makes a home feel rich is not the size of the kitchen, but the number of people who feel comfortable cooking there with you.

As you consider cost, it may help to gently question what you actually need to feel at home. How many rooms, how much stuff, how much private lawn? What might you be ready to trade for deeper connection and shared abundance?

Self-Assessment: How Might You Afford Community Living?

Money is only one dimension of this journey, but it is an important one. A little honest self-assessment goes a long way. Here are a few questions to reflect on:

- What do I currently spend on housing each month, including utilities, insurance, and property taxes or renter's insurance?
- Do I qualify for a mortgage, or is renting or co-owning more realistic at this time?
- How open am I to downsizing my private space in order to gain shared amenities?
- Am I willing to relocate to a less expensive region if the right community exists there?
- Could I keep a remote job or income stream while living in a lower-cost area?
- Would I consider an income-sharing or work-trade community, at least for a season of life?
- What skills could I bring that might be valuable to a community, such as childcare, building, gardening, cooking, or administration?

You do not need perfect answers, but writing down your honest responses will help you clarify which models and regions make the most sense to explore.

Getting Creative with Your Path

Once a community knows you and wants you there, surprising options can open. I have seen this again and again.

A member at Rachel Carson Ecovillage, for instance, was initially unable to afford buying a unit. Over time, as relationships deepened, the community created a subsidized lease-to-own option that allowed her to move in and gradually build equity.

I worked with one client for months trying to find a suitable option for his income level, which was not quite low enough to qualify for subsidized housing but also not great enough to buy a home outright. He finally came into conversation with Sawyer Hill Ecovillage in Massachusetts, though he knew he could not buy in alone. Through the community network, he was connected with two other people in a similar position. Together they co-purchased a home under a rent-to-own style agreement and are on track to become equal co-owners.

These stories have a common theme: first there was a fit in values and relationships, then creative financing followed.

Some paths to explore, once you have a strong mutual interest with a community, might include:

- Sharing a home with housemates instead of buying or renting alone
- Parking a tiny house or ADU on community land where that is allowed
- Offering specific skills in exchange for partial rent or dues reduction
- Joining as a renter first, then exploring shared equity or co-buying later
- Participating in a community business that provides a stipend and covers some costs
- Applying for low-income or subsidized units if the community has them
- Exploring community land trust models that lower entry costs

None of these are guaranteed. The point is that intentional communities are often willing to think creatively once trust has been built.

Examples of Affordable Community Experiments

A few communities in North America that explicitly weave affordability into their mission include:

- Jamaica Plain Cohousing in Massachusetts, which includes a mix of market-rate and affordable units in a vibrant urban neighborhood.
- Elderspirit Community in Virginia, a senior cohousing model that combines modest private homes with strong mutual support.
- Boulder Housing Coalition in Colorado, a network of housing cooperatives that provide below-market rents and shared governance.
- Veterans Off Grid in New Mexico, which focuses on creating low-cost, land-based housing for veterans.
- Stone Soup Cooperative in Chicago, which operates cooperative group houses with accessible rents.

There are many more. The point is not to memorize names, but to realize that people across the continent are already building mixed-income, intentional neighborhoods that share resources and reduce costs.

The Real Cost, and the Real Value

So, how much does it cost to live in an intentional community?

It depends. It depends on where you live, what kind of community you choose, what role you play in that community, and how you define "enough."

Some communities will absolutely be out of reach for many people financially. Others are more attainable than you might expect, especially if you are willing to be flexible about location, housing type, or lifestyle.

Perhaps an even more powerful question to hold alongside the spreadsheets is this one:

*What is the cost of **not** living in community?*

There is a cost to isolation, to chronic stress, to juggling everything alone. There is a cost to raising children without a village, to aging without neighbors who notice if you fall, to facing climate and economic uncertainty without shared resilience.

Intentional community is not only about lowering expenses. It is about investing in relationships, mutual care, and a more livable future. Even when it costs the same as, or slightly more than, a conventional home, many people find the value they receive in return is far greater.

You are not just buying a house. You are choosing a way of life.

FINDING A DIVERSE COMMUNITY

> "We may have all come on different ships,
> but we're in the same boat now."
> —Martin Luther King Jr.

One of the most common requests I hear from clients is:

I want to join a diverse community.

Usually what they mean is diversity in age, race, and socioeconomic background. Sometimes they want diversity of lived experience, but not necessarily diversity of worldview. For example, someone may imagine a politically progressive community with every skin tone represented—yet also expect alignment in values, culture, and communication style.

Diversity, like community itself, is more layered than it appears at first glance.

This chapter helps you navigate that complexity with honesty, compassion, and realism.

Why Diversity Matters (and Why It's Complicated)

Many people, especially those from minority backgrounds, want to feel safe and at ease in a community where others share aspects of their identity. That desire is valid. If you are the only Black person, the only queer person, the only elder, or the only young parent, it can be challenging to feel you belong.

At the same time, some people seek a kind of curated diversity. One that looks varied on the surface but remains comfortably aligned underneath.

A "rainbow" community where everyone still thinks, votes, and communicates in similar ways.

There is nothing wrong with acknowledging you want cultural fit. But it's also worth gently questioning:

Do I want diversity, or do I want familiar comfort sprinkled with visible difference?

The truth is:

Diverse communities—those with meaningful differences in age, race, worldview, class, ability, and culture—require a high degree of intentionality and skill. They are incredibly rich places to live, but they ask more of us. More curiosity. More humility. More listening.

An Honest Look at the Movement

If you scroll through an intentional community directory today, most photos still show white faces.

This is not because BIPOC communities don't exist—they absolutely do—but because the mainstream intentional communities movement in the US emerged overwhelmingly from white countercultural and back-to-the-land initiatives.

Meanwhile:

- Many Black, Indigenous, and immigrant communities have long-standing traditions of communal living, mutual aid networks, and village culture.
- These communities often were never labeled "intentional communities" because they were created out of necessity, culture, or lineage—not as lifestyle experiments.
- Economic barriers, land theft, discriminatory lending, racism, and social inequities have all limited access to land and housing, shaping who forms and joins intentional communities today.

When viewed through this lens, it becomes clear why most rural intentional communities in North America remain white-majority spaces.

This context is important, not to blame, but to understand what you're stepping into.

Communities Doing the Work

In recent years, conversations around racial justice, especially those sparked by the murder of George Floyd and the Black Lives Matter movement, have encouraged many intentional communities to look more closely at inclusion, access, and belonging. Most groups are still learning how to put these values into practice, while other groups already deeply embodied them.

One example is **Canticle Farm** in Oakland, California. I'll never forget turning off a crowded city street, slipping down an alley, and suddenly finding myself in a permaculture oasis. Colorful gardens, yurts, little ponds—an ecovillage haven right in the heart of an urban neighborhood! This community does incredible work "to heal and transform historical and present-day trauma across difference, especially that of race, gender, class, religion, and age." They host a range of programs, including a home for the formerly incarcerated, a home for youth activists, and numerous gift-economy-based gatherings.

Another is the **People's Network for Land and Liberation (PNLL)**, which focuses on land decommodification, self-determination, and community-based liberation movements. Their work challenges the economic roots of exclusion and invites people to imagine new models of shared land stewardship. They currently have centers developing in Mississippi, Massachusetts, and even one near where I live here in Vermont.

One more beautiful model to share is **Ekvn-Yefolecv** in Alabama, an Indigenous Maskoke intentional ecovillage founded by people returning to their ancestral homelands after more than 180 years of displacement. Their village is centered on linguistic, cultural, and ecological revitalization. In some areas of the community, only Maskoke is spoken.

Their message to those who want to help is simple: "Support our work indirectly through the commitment to adopt regenerative communal lifeways in [your] own bioregional contexts." It is a reminder that "diversity" does not always mean everyone mixes equally everywhere; sometimes it means safeguarding the sovereignty and continuity of a specific cultural group.

If you are seeking a specifically BIPOC-led or racially diverse community, the **BIPOC Intentional Communities Council** maintains an online directory that can be a helpful place to begin.

Culture First, Not Recruitment

Crystal Farmer, author of *The Token*, offers one of the most important teachings for communities and seekers alike:

Don't recruit diversity. Become the kind of culture where diversity naturally feels welcome.

This is crucial.

It is neither fair nor effective for a community to "collect" diverse members like decorative accents. Instead, a community must cultivate:

- Healthy conflict resolution practices
- Trauma-informed communication
- Cultural humility
- Awareness of power dynamics
- Anti-racist and anti-oppressive commitments
- A willingness to look inward, not outward, for change

A supportive environment attracts diverse people because the culture feels safe, not because the demographics have been engineered.

Urban vs. Rural: What to Expect

Generally speaking:

- **Urban communities** tend to have more racial and cultural diversity simply because cities are more diverse.
- **Rural communities** may reflect the demographics of the surrounding region.
- In areas with more racially diverse populations, communities tend to reflect that naturally.

- In homogeneous rural areas, a "diverse" community may still be predominantly white despite good intentions.

If you prioritize diversity, consider expanding your search to:

- Cities or peri-urban areas
- Regions with large BIPOC populations
- Communities explicitly centering racial justice or cultural revival
- BIPOC-led or BIPOC-majority communities
- Faith-based or interfaith communities (often more multigenerational and multi-ethnic)

A Wider Definition of Diversity

When community seekers focus only on race, they sometimes overlook:

- Age diversity
- Neurodiversity
- Family structure
- Ability and disability
- Socioeconomic background
- Cultural upbringing
- Citizenship or language
- Political worldview
- Gender and sexuality
- Religious or spiritual diversity
- Work style and communication style

In many cases, the most impactful diversity is invisible: values, worldview, and cultural assumptions that shape daily life.

A community with three different races but identical beliefs may feel less diverse than a monocultural community with broad ideological, generational, and class diversity.

Ask yourself:

What kind of diversity will help me feel more whole and more at home?

And what kind of diversity will challenge me in growthful ways?

Both matter.

If You Are a BIPOC or Marginalized Seeker

Your safety and comfort come first. Period.

Here are a few grounded suggestions:

- Pay close attention to how a community talks about race, inclusion, and equity.
- Ask who holds power and who is missing.
- Notice how people respond when you raise questions about belonging.
- Look for communities with more than one person of your background—not because numbers guarantee safety, but because it reduces the emotional burden of being "the first."
- Seek out BIPOC-led or BIPOC-majority communities if that feels important to you.
- Reach out to the BIPOC Intentional Communities Council for support and resources.

You deserve to feel seen, safe, and valued—not tokenized.

If You Are White and Want a More Diverse Community

A few suggestions:

- Focus on becoming a collaborative, humble, pro-equity neighbor—not on "finding" diverse people to join your dream.
- Be honest about your blind spots and willing to learn.
- Assess your community's culture: is it welcoming? trauma-informed? open to feedback?
- Consider the barriers: cost, location, style, communication norms, decision-making structures.
- Remember: affordability is a huge factor in racial diversity.

Communities that truly value diversity also value accessible entry.

How to Evaluate a Community's Culture around Diversity

Here are some reflective questions to guide your visits and conversations:

- Do people acknowledge issues of race, class, or power without discomfort or defensiveness?
- Does the group have clear agreements about inclusion and conflict?
- Are there written values around equity, access, or anti-oppression?
- Who is at the table? Who is not?
- How do they handle harm or microaggressions if they arise?
- Are BIPOC members in leadership roles—or bearing the emotional labor of educating others?

- Does the community partner with local organizations serving diverse populations?
- How do people talk about people who "aren't here"?
- Do you feel like your full self can breathe in the space?

Your body will often tell you more than any brochure.

Seeing Diversity through a Global Lens

Across the world, countless traditional villages, tribal communities, and diasporic groups live with strong cooperation, interdependence, and social cohesion. In many cases, these communities embody what Western intentional communities strive for—without ever using the term "intentional community."

It is often *privileged* cultures that have moved away from village life, wealth sharing, and interdependence.

This is worth remembering.

Sometimes the most "diverse" communities are not found in community directories at all. They are found in immigrant neighborhoods, religious communities, intergenerational households, and cultural enclaves with deep roots.

Final Thoughts: Finding Your Version of Belonging

Diversity is not a checkbox; it is a living dynamic shaped by real people with real histories. No community is perfect, and no community will match every hope you carry.

But there *are* communities striving to be inclusive, justice-oriented, welcoming, and reflective. There *are* BIPOC-led communities, intergenerational communities, queer-led communities, accessible communities, and culturally diverse communities that are eager to welcome the right people.

Your job is to get clear on:

- What kind of diversity matters most to you
- Where you feel safe and seen
- What you are ready to learn
- What you are ready to contribute
- How much stretch you can genuinely hold

You are not looking for a politically perfect place.

You are looking for a place where you can belong, grow, contribute, and feel at home.

FINDING COMMUNITY AS AN ELDER

"We are all just walking each other home."
—Ram Dass

A question I hear often from older adults is:

Am I too old to join an intentional community?

It's a fair question. Maybe you've dreamed of community living for decades and feel like the window has closed. Or perhaps this is a new idea—something stirred by a desire for connection, support, or meaning in your later years.

Here's the truth: **you are not too old.**

But age *does* shape your path, your options, and how communities respond to your inquiry.

This chapter explores what elders bring to community, what to expect when joining as an older adult, and how to find a place where you can age with dignity, contribution, and belonging.

Elders vs. "the Elderly": A Cultural Shift

Mainstream society tends to treat older adults as "the elderly." This phrase conjures frailty, decline, and burden. In contrast, many intentional communities prefer the word **elder**. The term carries reverence. Wisdom. Interdependence. Presence.

Communities like Elderspirit (Virginia) and Elderberry (North Carolina) even embed the identity into their name.

Intentional communities often model a social culture we've lost in the wider world. Instead of isolating seniors or pushing them into retirement villages where care is transactional, communities aim to create a fabric where every age is valued.

As Laird Schaub writes in "The Intergenerational Challenge," his article in *Communities* magazine (in the Spring 2015 issue), themed "Community for Baby Boomers":

"In community, we're trying to move deliberately away from defining security in terms of bank balances, and towards a wealth of relationship. In short, we're trying to address a major societal need without relying on a governmental safety net. Further, we want to do that with dignity, which generally means finding ways for everyone—young and old alike—to contribute meaningfully to the health of the whole."

In other words, community living restores what humans have practiced for most of our history: **intergenerational interdependence**.

Two Paths: Senior Communities vs. Intergenerational Communities

When exploring intentional community as an older adult, it helps to understand the two main models.

1. Senior Intentional Communities

These communities restrict the majority or all membership to seniors (with younger visitors always welcome). However, before you imagine the stereotypical Florida development, know that these communities are often far more vibrant and self-directed than the cliché "retirement communities" of golf carts and uniform houses.

In the United States, senior communities are exempt from certain provisions of the Fair Housing Act under the Housing for Older Persons Act (HOPA). This allows qualifying 55+ or 62+ housing to legally restrict residency based on age and to limit or exclude families with children.

Non-senior intentional communities or cohousing groups cannot restrict membership by age or exclude households with children unless they qualify under HOPA's strict criteria.

Key features of senior intentional communities:

- Seniors run the community themselves
- Residents collectively own their homes and common spaces
- Decisions are made by members, not outside management
- The community is designed for aging in place
- Accessibility features are built in from the start

Senior communities also tend to be straightforward to join, assuming:

- You can afford the home or buy-in
- A unit is available
- Your values align and you're ready to contribute

Resources for finding senior-focused communities include:

- **SageCohoAdvocates.org**
- **SeniorCoops.org**
- *The Senior Cohousing Handbook*

I often speak with older adults who start out wanting an intergenerational community, only to realize that not all mixed-age communities are designed with aging in mind. Accessibility, support, and culture vary widely. For some, this leads to choosing a senior community instead, simply because it offers more ease and better alignment with their needs.

And even in a senior community, you are not cut off from younger generations. Visiting friends and family, plus community events, still provide plenty of intergenerational connection.

2. Intergenerational Intentional Communities

This is where many older adults want to live.

They envision the quintessential village: made of laughing babies, working-age folks, wise elders, and everyone in between. They imagine supporting young families, sharing meals, being known by name, and offering mentorship and time.

Most intentional communities are intergenerational because this model reflects traditional village life—a social structure where every age has a role.

However, joining an intergenerational community as a senior comes with its own considerations.

Why Some Communities Become Top-Heavy

Even communities that deeply value elders sometimes face practical constraints. A village thrives when generations balance each other, but if many residents age in place while too few younger members join, the workload and care needs can become unbalanced.

This has happened in a number of communities founded in the 1960s and '70s. Many of their original members are now in their 60s, 70s, and 80s. Even newer communities are seeing an influx of older adults, who often have more financial resources and readiness to buy than younger seekers.

Findhorn, for example, now reports an average age of 55. And as *The Guardian* noted, communities like Bergholt Hall have begun curating membership to avoid becoming "top-heavy" with elders: *"Single applicants in their 50s and 60s (who represent over half of approaches) are likely to be disappointed."*

In the US, most communities cannot legally deny membership based solely on age unless they qualify as a senior community under HOPA. Still, communities with aging populations may try to attract younger folks by emphasizing affordability, family-friendly features, or leadership opportunities. Sometimes, elders even step back from central decision-making so younger residents can shape the community they're entering.

If you are over 60, you may have the best success with:

- Newer communities
- Communities in expansion phases
- Places actively seeking elders
- Communities without labor-intensive economic models
- Cohousing communities with clear and simple membership pathways

And if you're unsure, just ask. Communities will usually tell you what they're looking for.

If they say they are hoping to welcome younger people, take heart. While many communities want to balance their demographics, it is qualities like attitude, engagement, and relational style that matter far more than age. You may still thrive there, or in another community that is even more excited to welcome older residents.

Questions Seniors Should Ask When Evaluating a Community

As you move through the membership process, consider asking:

- What is the current age distribution?
- How do younger and older residents relate to each other?
- What accommodations exist for aging in place?
- Has the community supported elders through end-of-life care?
- What level of care can I realistically expect if I need help?
- How do seniors typically contribute?
- How does inheritance of homes or leases work here?

These questions help you understand not just the culture, but the future—potentially, your future.

What Communities Want from Older Prospective Members

Your age is just one factor among many. What matters most is your attitude:

Are you ready to contribute?

Communities are not looking for superhumans. They are looking for honest, engaged neighbors who want to be part of the whole.

Qualities communities appreciate in older members include:

Time
Younger adults often struggle to juggle work, kids, studies, and meetings. Retirees have more availability for community needs, making them invaluable.

Mentoring and Life Experience
You don't need a resume of special skills. Your lived experience is often more valuable than any formal training.

Committee Work
Many seniors shine here—research, admin, bookkeeping, governance, problem-solving.

Childcare Support
Parents in community often feel stretched thin. Elders can make daily life dramatically easier for young families.

Mediation and Conflict Skills
Your perspective can help de-escalate conflicts and bring calm to a room.

Resources
Not every senior has wealth, but some do. Communities may appreciate donations, loans, shared tools, or simply the gift of a well-stocked kitchen.

So, Are You Too Old? Absolutely Not.

People in their 50s, 60s, 70s, and even 80s join intentional communities every year. They thrive. They contribute. They find purpose and joy in ways they never imagined.

You may need to be selective about which communities fit your needs, but you are not too old.

In fact, **communities need elders**—for balance, for wisdom, for continuity, and for the culture of care that only comes through lived experience.

Intentional communities can offer models for how society might better care for its elders: aging in place with dignity, surrounded by supportive neighbors, held by relationships instead of institutions.

If the dream is in you, it's not too late.

RAISING CHILDREN IN COMMUNITY

> "We are only the trustees for those who come after us."
> —William Morris

For generations, we've used the phrase "it takes a village to raise a child," but where are the villages now? Few people in developed nations actually live in anything resembling a traditional village.

This villagelessness has profound impacts on families. Parents are exhausted, childcare costs are sky-high, and children spend much of their time isolated from the everyday life of adults. As mothers' advocate Beth Berry writes, "The majority of our mental load and emotional labor as modern-day mothers comes from constantly and creatively trying to piece together some semblance of a village. Stepping into roles meant to be filled by other village members."

In intentional communities, families are rediscovering what shared care and intergenerational life can feel like—not as a nostalgic ideal, but as a lived reality.

Families with children are often among the most desirable members a community can attract. They bring vitality, commitment, laughter, and a genuine sense of future. Yet, paradoxically, they can also be the hardest to recruit and retain.

This chapter explores what it's like to join or raise a family in an intentional community. We'll look at the gifts, the challenges, and the magic of watching children grow up surrounded by caring neighbors.

Why Communities Need Families

A community that wants to be intergenerational usually craves plenty of kids in the mix. Kids bring noise, spontaneity, play, and perspective. Their presence keeps everyone humble and grounded in what really matters.

For existing communities, attracting families also brings continuity. Parents who put down roots for their children tend to stay longer, participate in governance, and invest in the future of the place. Children themselves become bridges across generations—learning from elders, inspiring young adults, and connecting newcomers to the culture of belonging.

A healthy intergenerational community mirrors a healthy ecosystem: diverse ages, roles, and rhythms all nourishing one another.

The Challenge of the First Family

While families are highly sought after, they may hesitate to join if there aren't already children around. A community with no existing families can feel uncertain to parents who are wondering, *"Who will my child play with?"*

This can shift quickly. Kids grow up, new families move in, and the rhythm of community life evolves. Many established ecovillages go through natural waves—a lull with few children followed by a vibrant new cohort of births and young families.

For both newer and long-standing communities, however, attracting families can be challenging because the financial barriers we explored in earlier chapters often hit young parents hardest. Childcare expenses, tight budgets, and the sheer logistics of raising kids can make community living feel out of reach.

For parents visiting a community, it's worth asking not only *"How many kids live here now?"* but also *"How has that changed over time?"* and *"How might it change in the future?"*

Parenting in the Village

Parenting in community is profoundly rewarding and occasionally maddening. You are never alone, but you are also never invisible. Everyone sees your parenting style, and at times, everyone has an opinion about it. Parents often find that they have extra support but less privacy. A child may gain a dozen "aunties" and "uncles," but also a dozen sets of expectations. Conflicts between children can ripple through adult relationships, and the shared environment means learning how to set consistent boundaries together.

Parenting issues are among the most common sources of community tension. This is not a sign of failure. It is a sign of deep involvement. Healthy communities navigate these moments by keeping communication open and remembering that everyone is learning. Parents, children, and neighbors are all figuring it out together.

Some intentional communities began with much more communal approaches. Kibbutzim in Israel famously practiced collective childrearing, where children slept in children's houses rather than with their parents.

ZEGG in Germany experimented for years with shared parenting and collective responsibility for the next generation. Most of these radical models have since shifted toward more individual family structures, yet the legacy remains. They still maintain a strong co-parenting culture, with far more collaboration among adults than in most mainstream environments.

It Really Does Take a Village

When it works, raising kids in community can be profoundly life-affirming.

- **Shared care:** Elders and retirees often step in for childcare, tutoring, or companionship.
- **Peer support:** Parents swap babysitting, meals, and emotional backup during hard phases.
- **Role models:** Children grow up around a variety of adults—artisans, gardeners, builders, artists, elders—learning from real life, not just from screens.
- **Mixed ages:** Older kids mentor younger ones, reducing cliques and creating a sense of continuity.
- **Outdoor freedom:** Safe environments with minimal car traffic allow children to roam and explore.

Boundaries and Agreements around Kids

For families joining community, clarity around children's spaces and expectations can make or break the experience. Every group has a different comfort level about noise, mess, and supervision.

Questions to ask before joining:

- How many children currently live here, and what are their ages?

- Where are kids free to play, and where are quiet zones?
- How do we handle safety, supervision, and shared property?
- Are there shared childcare systems, homeschool groups, or family activities?
- How do you handle conflict between parents—or between kids—when it arises?

If a community already has families, ask the parents directly what it's *really* like. Their insights will tell you far more than a brochure.

Alloparenting in Community

Even though I'm not a parent myself, community life has given me a crash course in what it means to practice *alloparenting*, the traditional human pattern where many adults share responsibility for the children around them.

A good example is the small pond I built at the entrance of my home. I imagined it as a peaceful water garden with frogs, lilies, and the sound of a gentle waterfall. What I didn't imagine was everything that would unfold once the community kids discovered it!

Suddenly the stones became slippery under little feet, rocks were flying into the water, mud was splashing up the sides, and frogs were being captured with great enthusiasm and questionable gentleness. With no other parents around, I became the responsible adult by default. I found myself setting boundaries, redirecting behavior, coaxing kids away with promises of chocolate, and comforting a distraught child after a beloved doll took an unexpected plunge into the pond.

This pond has taught me more about children, and about my own patience, than any parenting book ever could. Alloparenting wasn't something I necessarily planned for when I joined this community, but it has become part of my day-to-day simply by living here.

Education and Learning Pathways

Most intentional communities value experiential and holistic education. You'd be amazed at how many are located near Waldorf, Montessori, or nature-based schools, or have organized homeschooling or unschooling groups on site. Others partner with local public schools and provide after-school or summer enrichment in gardens, workshops, or the arts.

A common pattern: younger children are homeschooled or attend alternative programs, while older kids integrate into nearby schools for extracurriculars or college prep.

In many intentional communities, children don't just *live* in a village—they learn from it.

In Costa Rica, for example, several ecovillages collaborate with the World School in San Mateo, a bilingual, nature-rooted program launched by ecovillage residents. Over time it has grown into a regional hub shared by neighboring communities like Alegría Village and La Ecovilla. Children from across the region carpool together and grow up together. At RISE Costa Rica, another ecovillage, families benefit from a Waldorf school right on-site, where lessons flow between classrooms, gardens, and forest trails.

In Canada, La Cité Écologique offers one of my favorite examples. It began as a summer camp for kids. The story I heard is that the kids loved the camp so much they begged their parents to create a more permanent version of that life. Miraculously, the parents agreed. Today, La Cité is a thriving ecovillage where the school remains central to daily life, open to both community children and those from surrounding towns.

And in Germany, Schloss Tempelhof has become well known for integrating education into the heart of the village. Their school is built on simple but profound questions: *What kind of environment helps a child unfold? How can learning be woven into real life?* Children there regularly join adults in hands-on projects: baking bread in the communal kitchen, welding in the metal shop, tending garden beds, or helping construct a tiny house. As Tempelhof likes to say, *"Our university is wherever the construction site is."* The whole village becomes a campus.

For families seeking a place where children grow within a rich social fabric, these communities demonstrate what's possible when education is not separated from life, but interwoven with it.

A Pattern Older than Schools

What places like Tempelhof embody is something architect Christopher Alexander described in *A Pattern Language* as "shopfront schools." In his vision, learning spaces are "dotted among the living functions of the community." Children wander in and out of workshops, gardens, kitchens, and studios, learning directly from adults who are deeply engaged in meaningful work.

This is the traditional way humans have educated children—through immersion, apprenticeship, and belonging. Modern life has separated learning from living, but intentional communities often recreate this pattern simply by virtue of their design, scale, and culture.

Alexander's work is an excellent resource for designing villages more broadly. His patterns describe not only buildings but relationships: how people move, gather, work, and care. His ideas have been a continual source of inspiration for me personally, especially in thinking about how communities can nurture the whole human, from childhood through elderhood.

Family Finances and Contribution

Parents are often stretched for time and energy. Communities that succeed with families understand this and offer flexibility: part-time workshares, rotating childcare, or reduced meeting loads during early parenting years.

If you're a parent joining a community, be upfront about your current capacity—and your desire to contribute when life allows. Most groups appreciate the honesty. They'd rather you be engaged in a sustainable way than over-commit and burn out.

Reflection Questions for Parents

- What kind of social environment do I want my child to grow up in?
- How much community involvement feels right for our family?
- How flexible am I with schooling options and structure?
- What support do I need as a parent right now?
- Am I ready to share both joys and challenges with my neighbors?

Raising children in community is not about perfection. It's about weaving life together—elders, parents, and kids co-creating a daily rhythm of mutual care.

You will make mistakes, your neighbors will too, and your children will witness real people learning to live cooperatively. That may be the greatest education of all.

The village is not an ideal. It's a practice, and our children are the reason we keep practicing.

JOINING A COMMUNITY ABROAD

> "We can view the search for a better world as exploration. We may discover that the expedition is the better world, and that our own most important discoveries will be along the lines of how to improve the expedition—how to get others to join and help in the search."
>
> —Willam S. Copperthwaite

For many people exploring intentional communities, the question may eventually arise:

What if my ideal community isn't in my country at all?

Maybe you've always dreamed of living closer to nature in a tropical climate. Maybe you're longing for a different political atmosphere, social fabric, or sense of freedom. Or maybe you simply feel called to live somewhere that aligns more deeply with your values.

Exploring intentional communities abroad can be a way to reimagine your life from the ground up—not just changing your address, but your culture, climate, pace, and people. It's one of the most life-expanding paths you can take, but also one that requires care, patience, and preparation.

Why Move Abroad for Community?

There are many motivations that lead people to seek community beyond their borders:

- **Climate:** You're drawn to year-round growing seasons or milder weather.
- **Politics:** You're ready for a more stable or values-aligned society.
- **Economics:** Lower living costs or fairer systems appeal to you.
- **Family:** You want to live near relatives or raise children in a safer, slower-paced environment.
- **Freedom:** You want to live outside the box of conventional expectations, perhaps even off-grid.
- **Adventure:** You're ready to experience life in a different culture and language.

What Joining Abroad Really Involves

Joining an intentional community abroad offers a chance to become part of places that are at the forefront of innovation, regeneration, and a renewed understanding of what it means to be a global citizen.

La Ecovilla in Costa Rica, for example, is well known for its regenerative design and its welcoming culture for international remote workers, with nearly thirty countries represented. Auroville in India is another well-known example: a spiritually-oriented international township with residents from more than fifty nations.

Visiting places like these can be inspiring. Joining them is a deeper commitment. You are not only choosing a community. You are choosing a country, a language, and an entirely new set of cultural, legal, and economic realities.

It helps to ask yourself a few honest questions:

- Have you lived or traveled abroad for more than a few weeks at a time?
- How do you respond to culture shock, language barriers, and unfamiliar systems?
- Which languages do you speak now, and which could you realistically imagine learning well enough to truly connect with people?
- Can you picture yourself navigating a full immigration process for this particular country?

If you are not sure yet, start with a visit. Explore a few intentional communities, but also spend time in the surrounding region. Communities often have cultures that feel quite different from life outside their borders, and you will want a sense of both. Most people discover that there is a big gap between reading about a community online and sitting at someone's kitchen table, walking the land, or watching how decisions are made. That experience reveals far more than any website ever could.

Immigration: What Changes and What Does Not

One of the biggest misconceptions I hear is that joining an intentional community abroad somehow changes the immigration rules. It usually does not. Communities may be able to advise you and write letters of support, but you are still subject to the laws of the country.

Most people begin their exploration as tourists. If you are an American or EU citizen, it is relatively easy to visit many countries for up to ninety days. That is how you will probably make your first visits to communities abroad. If you decide you want to stay longer, that is when you start looking at visas, such as extended tourist visas, student or volunteer visas, work permits, or self-employment visas.

If you decide that a country truly feels like home, you may eventually apply for residency or even citizenship. That process can involve proving a certain level of income, purchasing property, or meeting other requirements. In Costa Rica, for example, there are specific "pensionado" and "rentista" visas for retirees and people with guaranteed income. In India, Auroville has a special status as an international township that allows non-Indians to reside there through a dedicated "Auroville visa," although the specifics change and always need to be checked at the time you apply.

Many larger communities are experienced in walking people through what has worked for past residents. They can help you understand the likely pathways and pitfalls, but they cannot change the law. It is wise to combine their advice with your own research and, when needed, the help of an immigration attorney or relocation consultant. I also highly encourage joining country-specific online groups (like expat forums or Facebook communities). They're often the best source of up-to-date, lived experience for the particular country you are interested in moving to.

Learning the Language and the Culture

Language is one of the most underestimated pieces of moving abroad. Even if a community uses English internally, the surrounding society usually does not. It is not a problem for you to travel in most places around the world as an English-only speaker. Especially in Europe, especially younger generations, most people speak some English.

However, once you commit to moving to a country with a different language, it's important that you also commit to learning the language, both for the sake of your social well-being and as a sign of respect for the locals.

As our lead Costa Rica Ecovillage Tours Guide, Jason Thomas, shares, "When you make the effort to speak someone's language, you're communicating something profound: 'You are worth the effort. Your way of expressing yourself matters to me. I appreciate my welcome here and will do my best to honor it.' Nothing builds trust more quickly."

I had my own version of this lesson while living in an ecovillage in Slovenia. Slavic languages are not known for being easy. I could manage errands okay, and within the community there were plenty of English speakers. But at parties and broader social gatherings, people naturally reverted to their mother tongue. I found myself dependent on my immediate community for social connection, which is never a healthy long-term arrangement.

Eventually I realized I was not willing to devote the time and focus it would take to feel truly at home in that language, and that helped me decide not to root there permanently.

Culture is just as important. Many countries place a high value on manners and relationship-building. In Costa Rica, for example, it is common to greet people fully and ask how they are before getting down to business. In Germany, punctuality carries a strong meaning. In India, there can be intricate unspoken expectations around hospitality and cleanliness. I'll never forget the time I was at an outdoor cafe in Auroville and mistakenly rested the shoes I was holding on a table. A local diner saw me and angrily insisted I clean the table thoroughly, immediately.

None of this is about performing correctness. It is about learning how people show respect and care in that place.

Tips for a Smoother Transition

Before you commit to a permanent move, give yourself time to experiment.

If at all possible, pre-visit the community you are considering. Join a retreat, volunteer for a few weeks, or come on a guided tour. Pay attention not only to what the community says about itself, but how it feels to wake up there, to walk the paths, to interact with both residents and neighbors.

Ask whether the community uses your language for meetings, meals, and social events, or whether another language is primary. Even if most people speak English, will you be able to find work, friendships, and support outside the community, or will you be dependent on a small circle of bilingual friends?

Stay connected after you leave. Follow the community's social media pages, join their newsletters or online gatherings, and talk with alumni. They can often give a more rounded picture of life there over time.

If you can, consider spending a full year in the region before formally joining a community. The dry and rainy seasons, summer and winter, holiday periods and slow months each reveal something different about a place.

Money, Work, and Healthcare

Financial planning is one of the most practical and important aspects of joining a community abroad.

Some people keep their existing work by going remote. Communities like RISE in Costa Rica were designed with this in mind, offering coworking spaces, reliable internet, and a supportive environment for people whose income is still rooted in another country. Others find ways to earn locally, through teaching, trades, tourism, online businesses, or community-based enterprises. Some communities offer work-exchange arrangements that cover housing or part of your food costs in return for a set number of hours.

If you are retired or semi-retired, look closely at how your pensions or social security will function abroad. Many countries offer special visas for retirees, but each has its own rules about income levels and proof.

Healthcare is another key piece. Some countries, such as Costa Rica and Portugal, have strong public healthcare systems that residents can access affordably once they obtain the right legal status. Others rely more on private clinics and insurance. In India or Bali, for example, there is excellent medical care available in many cities at a fraction of North American prices, but you will probably want private insurance and to research specific hospitals in advance.

You may want to maintain bank accounts in your home country for a time, even if you open local accounts as well. Tax obligations can continue even after you move, especially for US citizens, so it is wise to understand this early rather than be surprised later.

Part-Time Community Living

Not everyone is ready, or able, to move abroad full-time. Living part-time in a community overseas can be a way to explore this lifestyle without giving up your home base.

Some people spend winters in a Costa Rican community and summers in North America or Europe. Others rotate between a village in Portugal and family in their country of origin. This can reduce financial and emotional pressure and make it easier to maintain healthcare and social ties at home.

Part-time living can also simplify visas. In the Schengen area of Europe, you can stay for ninety days within any one hundred eighty day period.

In Costa Rica, tourists can stay for up to ninety days, then reset their time with a short trip abroad. These rules change and have nuances, so always check current regulations, but in many places shorter, regular stays are more straightforward than full residency.

However, not all communities welcome part-time residents. Some are designed for a stable, year-round population and need consistent participation. Others, such as Traditional Dream Factory in Portugal, are intentionally geared toward nomadic or seasonal members. Always find out how a community handles comings and goings, and whether subletting or shared ownership is allowed.

Finding the Right Fit

Some countries are known for being especially welcoming to foreigners. Costa Rica, Portugal, and Thailand all have strong expat networks and multiple intentional communities. Mexico, Greece, and parts of Eastern Europe are also attracting more projects and seekers.

Within any country, certain communities are more international than others. Larger ecovillages and older projects tend to have more global diversity and more experience integrating people from different backgrounds. In those settings, English is often used as a common language in meetings and gatherings, even if several other languages are spoken as well.

Places like Findhorn in Scotland, Tamera in Portugal, Auroville in India, Sekem in Egypt, EcoVillage at Ithaca in the United States, Sieben Linden in Germany, and Damanhur in Italy are all examples of larger, well-established projects that host visitors from around the world. Even if you do not plan to live in one of these communities, visiting them can be incredibly educational.

When you are evaluating a specific community abroad, look beyond the photos. Especially in areas of the world with increased gentrification, you can become part of the solution and not worsen the problem through a careful analysis of a community's relationships with locals.

Some questions to ask a potential community:

- Who lives there now? How long have people stayed? What is the mix of local and international residents?
- How do you relate to nearby towns and villages? Listen to hear how they describe themselves as part of the local fabric, or separate from it. Do you hear more about partnership with neighbors, or more about frustration and criticism?
- How has your approach changed over time? Usually expat communities can describe lots of lessons they've learned through interactions with locals over the years. Listen closely for an attitude of learning and respect.

Making the Decision

Ultimately, the decision to join an intentional community abroad is deeply personal.

It can help to sit with a few reflective questions.

- Am I seeking this move mainly to get away from something, or because I feel genuinely called toward a particular place or way of life?
- How do I respond to uncertainty and slow processes?
- Can I see myself learning a new language enough to function kindly in daily life?
- How would this move affect my children, parents, or close relationships?
- What resources, inner and outer, do I have to navigate the harder parts?

If you feel drawn in this direction but are not ready to commit, start small and concrete.

Join an Ecovillage Tour (**ecovillagetours.com**) as an excellent way to get broad exposure to different communities in a particular region. Then you can return for a longer stay or to volunteer with a project you admire. Stay long enough that the initial honeymoon wears off and you can see some of the cracks.

Many people who travel with us do not end up moving abroad right away, yet the experience still changes them. Once you know in your bones that these ways of living really exist, your choices back home begin to shift. You may start a small shared housing project, join a local co-op, or plan a longer sabbatical to explore.

There is no one right path. There is only the path that fits you, in this season of your life.

Wherever you go, remember that community is not something you buy. It is something you help create through your presence and your daily choices. Whether you stay for a season or for a lifetime, you have the opportunity to be not just a consumer of a beautiful place, but a co-creator of a living village.

PART V:

STARTING A COMMUNITY

SHOULD YOU START A COMMUNITY?

> "Ours is not the task of fixing the entire world all at once, but of stretching out to mend the part of the world that is within our reach."
>
> —Clarissa Pinkola Estes

The decision to start an intentional community is not one to take lightly. While exact statistics are hard to verify, we can assume the failure rate of new communities mirrors that of business start-ups: high, costly, and painful for would-be founders.

And yet, the world needs more intentional communities!

We need places where neighbors support each other, where people work together to enrich the land they call home, and where resilience, trust, and belonging grow.

At the same time, we also need more people to join the communities already seeking members.

There are now hundreds of intentional communities in various stages of development. Nearly every US city or town I've researched has at least one forming group toying with the idea of cooperative housing. Perhaps you can join forces with a group already underway.

If you feel a strong pull to start something completely new, that impulse deserves careful attention.

The path is long and challenging, yet easier than ever before. The process of founding a community is far more documented than it once was, with resources, consultants, and frameworks that simply didn't exist decades ago.

Two Main Pathways into Community

If you crave a life in community, there are two main paths to get there:

1. **Start a community from scratch (the founder path).**
2. **Find an existing community to join (the finder path).**

Both paths can be meaningful. Both can stretch you in ways you cannot anticipate. People often shift between these roles as their life circumstances change.

When I launched my membership program, the Community Circle, we originally created two separate tracks: one for **founders** and one for **finders**. Over time it became clear that most people in the early stages move back and forth between these roles. Sometimes people think they want to start a community, then learn more about what already exists, decide to join something, live there for a while, and even eventually come full circle to wanting to create something new.

We eventually folded the two tracks into one, because the early steps for finding and founding are so similar. Both paths begin with research, visiting communities, and learning what is possible. Having everyone in one group also creates richer learning. Founders get to pitch their community ideas to real people seeking community, and finders receive guidance that helps them join a diversity of communities with more confidence.

So how do you know which path is right for you?

This chapter will help you explore that question.

Clarify What You Actually Want

Before deciding anything, take time to understand what you are truly looking for. Revisit the chapter on **Creating a Community Wishlist**—it's just as valuable for founders as it is for finders.

Write down the location, values, lifestyle, and community patterns that feel important to you. Let yourself be a little idealistic at this stage. Name what is non-negotiable and what is flexible.

Later, you will refine this list as you learn more about what is possible, what you can adapt to, and what genuinely matters.

You can even share your Wishlist with cofounders or early members. Consider gathering a small group and inviting everyone to develop their own Community Wishlists, both individually and together. Over time, these early lists may even become the foundation for your community's guiding documents.

Research Existing Communities

Once you know what you want, begin exploring the communities that already exist. One of the most common mistakes aspiring founders make is assuming no community matches their vision. Often this assumption comes from limited research.

Spend time reading about communities that interest you. Reach out to them. Have conversations. And, most importantly, **visit them**.

It is difficult to imagine starting a community if you have not experienced real ones firsthand. Every visit offers lessons, whether the community aligns with your Wishlist or not. Sometimes you discover that a lifestyle you thought you wanted doesn't fit you after all. Other times, you find a place that surprises you with a sense of home you didn't expect.

Yana Ludwig, author of *Building Belonging*, tells a story about imagining herself in a secluded cabin in the woods. When she finally lived that way, she realized she actually craved more social energy. That experience shifted her vision completely. Without visiting, she might have built a community she later disliked.

Sometimes your ideal community ***does*** exist—just not in the location you need it to be. We are often tied to places through work, family, or existing social networks. Maybe you even have the land you want to build a community on already.

Still, go visit the models that inspire you elsewhere. Speak with their founders about what it would take to re-create something similar in your region. Ask whether they'd be open to advising you as you go.

Also seek out communities near you, even ones that don't match your Wishlist. Network with their founders. Often the communities closest to you can reveal start-up groups, local resources, and unexpected pathways: which planning commissioner to befriend, where affordable land might be listed, or whether there's a vacant building just right for a new chapter in community living.

If you're unsure where or how to visit communities, see the previous chapter on **Visiting Communities**.

Assess Your Energy and Time

Starting a community requires a level of dedication that can surprise people. It is far more than a full-time job in the beginning and will require ongoing energy for years. Depending on the size and complexity of your vision, be prepared for two to seven years (or more!) of consistent focus.

Ask yourself:

- Do I have the capacity to lead a complex, long-term project?
- Can I make space for this without pushing aside health, family, or other commitments?
- Is my desire to found a community stronger than my desire for immediate stability?

There may be other ways to fulfill your purpose in the world that do not require the same level of strain.

I cannot tell you how many times I have daydreamed about starting a community.

I have plenty of energy for start-up projects, but I also know I operate best from a relaxed and stable environment. In the end, I chose to compromise on a few pieces of what my ideal community might look like in order to join an established one. This allowed me to give my energy to other projects, such as running Ecovillage Tours and writing this book.

Maybe you also have a book in you, or a nonprofit to create, or a family to start. It is certainly possible to take on more than one big endeavor at a time, but is it the wisest choice for you? Is there a timeline or order of operations that would let you accomplish all your dreams without burning out? What is most important to focus on first?

These questions are worth reflecting on honestly before you choose the founder path.

Consider Your Skills and Your Future Team

Communities are not built by lone visionaries. They are built by small teams of committed people with complementary skills. Early on, a community stops being "your project" and becomes "our project."

Ask yourself:

- Am I comfortable sharing leadership?
- Who might join me as a fellow founder?
- Do I bring essential skills such as communication, organization, or conflict navigation?

We'll dive deeper into how to develop your skills and gather a founding team in the next chapter. For now, just assess your willingness to do the work.

Explore Your Motivations

It is important to examine why you want to start a community. This is not about judging yourself but about understanding what is driving your desire.

Are you seeking belonging? Influence? Healing? Purpose?
Are you imagining a community that corrects something missing in your past?
Are you drawn to leadership or to collaboration?

A healthy ego is useful. An inflated ego can quietly undermine the entire project. Be honest with yourself. Make sure your vision serves a community, not only yourself.

A Middle Path: Joining a Forming Community

If you are torn between founding and joining, consider a third option: joining a group still in early formation. This path lets you participate in shaping the community without carrying the full burden of being a founder.

You still get to influence culture, policy, and direction, but with shared responsibility. For many people, it offers the creativity they crave without the overwhelm.

Forming communities can be harder to find, yet they do exist. Look online for regional groups, discussion forums, and Facebook communities. Explore nearby towns. Read every flyer in local cafes, libraries, yoga studios, and food co-ops. Check for MeetUp groups or nonprofits connected to community living. Local environmental organizations, such as sustainability or conservation groups, can also be strong leads. Attend their workshops, stop by their offices, and see what you can learn.

Which Path Is Right for You?

If you reach the end of this reflection and still feel energized, clear, and determined, the founder path may be yours. The world does need more courageous, thoughtful people willing to build new models of living.

But do not underestimate the power of joining a community that already exists. Joining is often the faster, wiser, and more supportive path. Many people discover that what they truly desire is not to build a community but to live in one.

Whichever path you choose, remember that the goal is the same:

A life of connection, contribution, and belonging.

In the next chapter, we will explore practical advice for those who feel strongly called to start a community and want to understand what comes next.

ADVICE FOR STARTING A COMMUNITY

> "There is no power for change greater than a community discovering what it cares about."
> —Margaret J. Wheatley

By now, you may have decided that you want to start an intentional community. You understand the challenges and the time horizon. You recognize the difference between the founder path and the finder path. And even with that clarity, something in you says, "Yes. This is my work."

This chapter is here to help you take your first steps wisely.

Learn from the People Who Have Done It

Granted, this is one chapter on a topic that entire books are dedicated to teaching. I strongly encourage you to read those books.

Diana Leafe Christian's classic *Creating a Life Together* is an excellent starting point, as is Yana Ludwig's more recent *Building Belonging*. You will also find a wide variety of courses, workshops, and online events that can deepen your understanding.

If you are serious about this path, I recommend working with professionals who know this landscape well. Depending on your model, there are regenerative real estate advisors, cohousing consultants, and development groups that specialize in community-based projects. Here are some to explore:

- CoHousing Solutions
- The Cohousing Company
- CoVision Consulting
- Latitude Regenerative Real Estate
- New Earth Development
- CLIPS (Community Learning Incubator)
- Gaia Education (Ecovillage Design Course)

An updated list of groups and resources, along with their website links, can be found at **communityfinders.com/book1**.

These services are not inexpensive, yet they can prevent costly mistakes and shorten your learning curve.

The reality is that most forming communities never reach the point of purchasing land. Community projects tend to falter not because the vision was poor, but because founders were inexperienced, resources were insufficient, or interpersonal dynamics were unable to cope with the strain of a long and stressful process.

The goal of this chapter is to ground you with the tools and expectations that successful founders consistently rely on. It is not a substitute for the more extensive resources listed above, but it can serve as your early-stage survival guide.

Build Experience Before You Build a Community

I may start to sound redundant here, but if there is one universal piece of advice from every founder I have ever met, it is this: spend meaningful time living in community before trying to start one.

Even a short-term residency or work-exchange experience can give you a realistic view of the daily rhythms, governance structures, and interpersonal dynamics involved. You will learn far more from observing one real conflict resolution process than from reading twenty articles about conflict resolution. You will understand how membership decisions actually unfold, what happens during stressful periods, and how shared responsibilities get distributed.

This embodied experience will become the foundation of your judgment as a founder.

The Steps to Community Creation

The steps below assume you envision a full-fledged settlement. If you're looking to retrofit a small building or already have a space for community, it's likely the steps below will be shorter and more straightforward for you.

Below is a high-level roadmap of the steps most intentional community founders move through. The steps are not necessarily linear, and some, like clarifying your motivations or researching other community models, will continue throughout every phase.

Phase 1: Personal Clarity

Months 0 to 1

- Clarify your motivations and long-term vision.
- Create your Community Wishlist.
- Assess your energy, time, and personal capacity.
- Continue to visit multiple communities to understand what works in real life.

Phase 2: Early Visioning and Research

Months 1 to 3

- Draft a simple vision statement.
- Research community models, legal structures, and local zoning realities.
- Identify whether you lean toward cohousing, cooperative living, ecovillage, land trust, or another structure.
- Begin networking with experienced founders, consultants, and advisors.
- Explore potential geographic locations.

Phase 3: Forming the Core Group

Months 3 to 6

- Meet people who share your values and goals.
- Host gatherings or online conversations to explore alignment.

- Invite a small group to create their own Community Wishlists.
- Begin discussing group norms and culture.
- Establish decision-making agreements for the early stage.

Phase 4: Vision to Concept

Months 6 to 12

- Co-create foundational agreements, such as mission, values, and membership expectations.
- Begin exploring legal and financial models.
- Take a community-building or cohousing training together.
- Start outlining budget needs and early financial commitments.
- Conduct feasibility research, including land availability and local regulations.

Phase 5: Pre-Development

Year 1 to 2

- Form a legal entity (many groups choose a limited liability company [LLC], cooperative, nonprofit, or HOA structure).
- Open a shared bank account with clear protocols.
- Refine membership pathways and roles.
- Begin conversations with architects, planners, real estate agents, and financial professionals.
- Identify land options and complete site visits.

Phase 6: Land Acquisition

Year 2 to 3

- Secure financing or member investment commitments.
- Make an offer on land or property.
- Complete due diligence: soil tests, surveys, zoning checks, environmental assessments.
- Purchase the land when all conditions are favorable.

Phase 7: Development and Building

Year 3 to 5

- Work with architects, builders, planners, and consultants.
- Finalize site design, utilities, housing layouts, and budget.
- Navigate permitting and regulatory approvals.
- Begin construction of homes, shared facilities, and site infrastructure.
- Continue welcoming new members.

Phase 8: Move-In and Culture-Building

Year 4 to 6

- Members move onto the land in phases.
- Create systems for governance, conflict resolution, maintenance, and shared responsibilities.
- Celebrate milestones together and refine community culture.
- Adjust agreements as needed to support real-world living.

Phase 9: Long-Term Stewardship

Year 6 and beyond

- Maintain land, buildings, and community systems.
- Welcome new generations of members.
- Continue developing shared projects, social life, and governance structures.
- Evolve as the community grows and matures.

But Wait, I Already Have Land!

Already have sprawling acreage or an old mansion that seems perfect for community life? Tired of running the homestead on your own or with just your family? Maybe you just closed on an RV park that would make the ideal setup for a tiny house ecovillage.

Plenty of intentional communities begin with founders who already own the land.

There are pros and cons to this path, just as there are pros and cons to doing a property search as a group.

Since you already have land and perhaps even basic infrastructure, you can often move much faster than a group that is still touring properties together. You will also have more control over who joins and how the early stages unfold on "your land."

But the drawbacks are worth acknowledging.

You will need to build community from the ground up. Anyone who joins will arrive with heightened awareness of potential power imbalances. Many would-be cofounders want to participate in the early-stage incubation, visioning, and property search. They may hesitate to join a project that already has these decisions locked in. Or, who knows, you might call in exactly the people you need!

Some intentional communities remain under founder ownership for their entire existence. When this works, there are clear and transparent boundaries around what decisions belong to the founder and what decisions belong to the group. These communities also tend to be more transient, since the founder becomes the anchor and sometimes the only long-term resident.

More often, founders set out with the intention of transitioning to group ownership. If this is your plan, articulate it clearly to prospective members and share a real timeline.

Too often the founder holds on too long while waiting for the right people, and the potential right people are never given the trust or authority to step in and prove themselves.

Consider how you could begin to build trust. Do you need a creative membership process? Could you live with people for a trial period? Complete a training together? Go on a camping trip? Build a dwelling?

For many founders, this trust-building process involves creating a legal structure where they retain a percentage of ownership. Other models allow monetary contributions or sweat equity to gradually buy the founder out. And some founders simply choose to gift their property to the community. That is a brave and generous choice.

It is also quite common for founders to eventually leave the communities they built. Power dynamics can become difficult to balance, and sometimes the most elegant solution is for the founder to step away. In other cases, the visionary founder feels out of place or even bored once the community is established. Sometimes they are asked to leave. Sometimes they go long before it reaches that point.

Yet I also meet founders who have learned the graceful art of staying involved without meddling. It is impressive to witness. They started the whole thing, yet they remain humble, non-attached, and deeply respected.

Remember, the community you are creating is like a child. You can help shape its early years, but who it grows up to be is ultimately out of your hands.

Forming a Strong Founding Circle

Regardless of whether you already have land, no one can build a community alone. It would be a contradiction of terms, after all.

The moment the first person joins, your vision becomes a shared vision. A forming community is a collaboration among people who bring different strengths, and it requires a founding circle that communicates well and shares responsibility.

Yana Ludwig recommends a founding group of three to eight people for most projects. This size balances diversity with manageability. Too few people and the workload becomes overwhelming. Too many people and decision-making becomes slow and murky.

Your group will need people who can hold big-picture vision, manage logistics, navigate conflict, organize meetings, handle money, recruit new members, and work with land and buildings. You do not need to excel in every area, but someone in your circle does. A healthy group also has the emotional maturity to give and receive feedback, stay transparent, and adjust roles as the project evolves.

As you form your founding circle, notice how well you are able to release control. Founders must adapt as others join, shifting from "my project" to "our community." Your circle will need clear roles, shared agreements, and a commitment to learning alongside one another.

Yana Ludwig captures this complexity well in *Building Belonging*:

"Starting a community is not like other activist projects, nor is it simply about being a good neighbor. Starting a community is a little like starting a nonprofit (because of the deep mission and passion work), starting a small business (because of the need for business and legal savvy), getting married (because of the intense relational work involved), and doing a really intense and long-term personal growth course (because, well, it is one). All at the same time. With the same group of people."

Yana goes on to question the would-be founder:

"Most of us have folks in our lives we might trust to start a business with, but are they the same people we trust to do intense and vulnerable relational and personal growth work with? And are those people the same ones with whom we share deep passions and an analysis of what the world needs? And do they want to live in the same places you are interested in living?"

If no one immediately comes to mind as a good fit for your founding team, do not fear. There are many ways to expand your network and call in future cofounders. Read on for my advice.

How to Find the People

Thanks to the internet and the growing interest in intentional communities, there are now more ways than ever to find people. The challenge is not finding many people. It is finding the *right* people.

The right people for you will depend on your needs, the gaps in your skills, and the values you want your members to embody. Get clear about your ideal cofounders and early members. How will you know if someone is a good fit? Why might you say yes or no?

Before you publish anything online about the project, create a simple onboarding pathway. Map it out step by step.

- Someone hears about you. *Then what?*
- They visit your website, community directory listing, or social media page. *Then what?*
- They fill out a contact form with a few basic questions. A simple Google Form works perfectly. *Then what?*
- You follow up and invite them to a scheduled public online session or, if they are local, an in-person meetup.

Have all of this in place and test it. Be prepared to handle dozens of inquiries.

Craft your landing page with honesty and care. Unless you're intentionally going for a certain vibe, I recommend including photos of yourself with other people—ideally smiling and engaged in shared activities. Images of site plans, aerial views, or even simple architectural sketches can help visitors imagine the future you're building.

In your text, offer a clear and grounded vision, while acknowledging that it will evolve as new members join. Name your non-negotiables. Describe who you are calling in. List the values that matter most. And if you have a preferred region or location, make sure to say so.

Then, when you are ready, share it widely.

Create listings on all the online directories mentioned in previous chapters. Most are free, and paid promotion on these same directories can be a good investment. You can also post about your project in social media groups, private chat channels, and online forums.

Go to **communityfinders.com/book1** for a comprehensive list of places where you can share your community project.

Always link back to one central place. Ideally this is a website with your own domain name, but it can also be a simple Google Form. The important thing is that you have a single place for people to learn more and offer their information.

The emails you collect during this stage are gold. They become the foundation of your audience. These are the people who may follow your project for years, sometimes silently, sometimes as donors, allies, or future members.

If you are trying to recruit in a specific location, do not underestimate the value of flyers. Post them in libraries, cafes, gyms, and other gathering spaces. Again, offer one simple way for people to learn more—a way that doesn't involve you responding to individual phone calls or emails.

And do not forget your existing relationships. Think of who you already know who might be ready for this kind of adventure. Perhaps an old college roommate who once dreamed about starting a commune. A relative with time and resources. Someone you met at a communication workshop who happens to live nearby.

If you are more introverted, it is even more important to team up with connectors. These are people with big networks and big personalities who can draw the right attention to your project.

With each conversation, each email, and each new connection, you are already weaving the beginnings of your community.

How to Find Funding

Most founders do not begin with deep pockets or access to large amounts of capital. If you do happen to have substantial financial resources, you may not need the strategies listed here, though you might consider how your funding could support not only your project but the wider ecosystem of intentional communities.

For everyone else, know this: communities don't fail because they lack vision (they usually have that in spades!). They *do* fail because they run out of runway.

Founders need realistic financial and energetic resources. Legal support, engineering, surveys, and design work costs accumulate long before any building begins. Even low-infrastructure models require steady funding for meetings, administration, and planning.

The good news is that there are strategies to get funding. No single approach is best. Most successful projects use a combination of several strategies that align with their values and limitations. Below are the most practical and realistic methods that real communities use to finance their beginnings.

1. Member Equity
Most projects begin with member contributions. These may take the form of early buy-in fees, periodic contributions, or sweat equity. Member equity creates shared commitment and helps identify who is genuinely ready to participate. Some groups use tiered or sliding-scale models so that people with different financial capacities can join.

2. Values-Aligned Lenders
There is a growing ecosystem of lenders who understand cooperative development and regenerative projects. Community development financial institutions (CDFIs), credit unions, ethical investment funds, and foundations offering program-related investments often provide more flexible terms than traditional banks. They typically want to see a clear mission, well-defined governance, and realistic financial planning.

3. Cooperative Financing Models
Cooperative ownership allows a group to collectively own land or buildings without requiring individual members to purchase private property. Housing co-ops, limited-equity co-ops, and community investment cooperatives keep housing affordable and prevent speculation. Members purchase shares rather than real estate, and the cooperative holds the underlying asset.

4. Community Land Trusts

A community land trust (CLT) holds land permanently for community benefit. Members lease the land at affordable rates while the trust keeps it out of the speculative market. Some communities create their own CLT, while others partner with an established one. CLTs also open the door to grants and public funding streams that require a nonprofit backbone.

5. Grants and Philanthropy

Grants rarely fund an entire community, but they can support important pieces such as agricultural work, environmental restoration, educational programs, or affordable housing components. Many communities receive grants through partnerships with nonprofits, municipalities, universities, or land trusts. These partnerships can strengthen a project's credibility and long-term resilience.

6. Municipal Partnerships

Local governments sometimes support intentional communities when they align with community needs such as workforce housing, sustainability goals, senior living, or neighborhood revitalization. This support may include zoning flexibility, long-term leases, access to public land, reduced permit fees, or help applying for grants. These partnerships take persistence but can be highly fruitful.

7. Mission-Aligned Investors

Some communities begin with help from a benefactor or impact investor. This can accelerate early development, but it is important to clarify expectations and create agreements that protect group autonomy. Shared governance, transparent terms, and clear exit plans help maintain balance.

8. Earned Revenue and Social Enterprise

Many communities operate small businesses that help fund operations and provide income for members. Examples include retreat centers, farms, educational programs, eco-tourism, maker spaces, or wellness services. The key is to start small and build capacity over time. A modest income stream can steady a project during early phases.

Funding a community is not about securing one large pot of money. It is about weaving together people, values, structures, and financial tools that can grow alongside your vision. Communities that succeed don't always start wealthy. They start organized, aligned, and determined, with a willingness to learn and adapt.

Prioritize Invisible Structures

Don't let the first conversations of your founding group be about the design of the fruit orchard!

Start with the invisible structures. These are the elements that hold the community together and allow everything to function. Focus early on your:

- Decision-making process
- Legal structure
- Conflict resolution process
- Financial plan
- Membership pathway, both for joining and leaving

Every community needs a clear decision-making system long before it owns land. Whether you choose voting, consensus, sociocracy, or something entirely new you make up, a clear process prevents confusion and protects relationships. For groups just starting out, the book *Who Decides Who Decides?* by Ted Rau will help you answer that very first question.

You will also need a simple and effective conflict resolution process. This does not mean avoiding conflict. It means creating a culture where conflict is expected, welcomed as a teacher, and handled with skill. A basic structure might involve direct conversation first, then support from a care team, and outside facilitation if needed.

Prospective members want to know how to engage with your project, so create a clear pathway for inquiry, information sessions, participation, and membership decisions. It does not need to be perfect, but it should exist. A pathway signals readiness and helps people understand what commitment looks like.

Transparency matters. People will want to see your agreements, your financial plan, your governance model, and your expectations. The more clarity you offer, the more trust your project will build.

The upcoming chapters will go deeper into the invisible structures communities commonly utilize.

A Few Early Practices That Make a Difference

Here are practices that new founders often find helpful, expressed as narrative guidance rather than checklists:

Begin by gathering your founding circle regularly. Meet at least once a week for relationship-building and planning. Use this time to ground yourselves in your purpose and to clarify your first steps. Start a shared document where you record decisions. This provides continuity during periods of change.

Start building your shared culture now. Remember each other's birthdays, celebrate a few holidays together, and host potlucks if you live nearby. Offer help with pet sitting, travel planning, or creative projects. If you do not live close to one another, plan a fun outing or a retreat. Do communication trainings together, but also try things like salsa dancing classes, whitewater rafting, or a group camping trip. Have fun together and build genuine bonds.

Outline your early roles. Even provisional roles bring structure and reduce confusion. Revisit these roles every few months as your needs shift. Start growing an interest list. People may not join right away, but they will appreciate being kept informed.

Once your group feels stable, discuss what kind of legal structure will best support your community. Diana Leafe Christian's work is especially helpful for comparing options such as cooperatives, LLCs, community land trusts, and homeowners associations. Your choice will depend on your values, financial model, and land plan.

Begin researching land-use requirements in the region you're considering building. Research zoning, density limits, water access, environmental permitting, and building codes. Many projects stall because they choose land without understanding the regulatory context. This is an area where working with a consultant can save significant time and money.

Most importantly, check in with one another often. Notice how you are doing emotionally. Community work pushes people to their edges. Supporting each other with care and honesty strengthens your foundation.

Founding as Inner Work

Starting a community is an invitation to grow. Your gifts will shine and your edges will be revealed. This work will ask for patience, humility, courage, and emotional resilience. Build practices that support your grounding. Seek mentors. Let yourself be changed by the process.

As Yana Ludwig writes, an unhealthy ego believes it is destined to save the world. A healthy ego helps you navigate challenges without collapsing.

Your vision does not need to be perfect or heroic. It needs to be honest and held lightly.

If You Remember Only a Few Things

Visit communities before you build one.
Strengthen your founding circle.
Establish your invisible infrastructure early.
Secure people and process before land.
Keep your purpose central and let the form evolve.
Enjoy each other's company.

Your Next Steps

The chapters ahead will explore legal, governance, conflict, and communication models in more depth.

For now, take your time, seek mentors, read widely, and continue building relationships. This work is both demanding and deeply rewarding. If you approach it with curiosity and a willingness to learn, you will not only increase your chances of creating a successful community. You will also grow in ways that prepare you to steward that community once it exists.

You are laying the groundwork for something meaningful. Take it step by step. I am cheering you on.

Expect a Long Timeline

Most community projects take between two and seven years to move from initial idea to actual move-in. Projects that involve raw land, extensive development, or challenging permitting environments often take even longer.

Allow this timeline to shape your expectations. You will need space in your life for meetings, research, due diligence, relationship-building, visioning, financial modeling, and the emotional ups and downs that come with collaborative creation.

Your early months will involve forming your group, choosing a governance model, clarifying your purpose, outlining a membership pathway, and deepening your relationships. Later phases involve entity formation, budgeting, land search, and due diligence. Only after those pieces are in place will you move toward design, construction, or renovation. And throughout, you will be communicating with prospective members and building a culture.

A generous buffer of time, energy, and money will make the journey smoother.

PART VI:

PREPARING FOR COMMUNITY

HOW DO COMMUNITIES WORK?

> "So, open your mouth, lad! For every voice counts!"
> —Dr. Seuss

When people first visit an intentional community, they may notice gardens, shared kitchens, networks of footpaths connecting a myriad of structures. But beneath all lies a quieter structure holding everything together—an invisible structure—the agreements, decisions, and legal foundations that make communal life possible.

A healthy community, like a healthy body, depends on the systems you can't always see. There's the **skeleton**—the legal and ownership structure that supports everything. There's the **nervous system**—the communication and decision-making pathways that send signals between members. And there's the **circulatory system**—the flow of resources, money, and energy that keeps the whole thing alive.

When all three work in harmony, a community can thrive for decades. When they're out of balance, even the most inspired projects can stumble. So, let's look a little deeper at what makes intentional communities actually *work* so you can recognize healthy systems when you see them, and perhaps help build new ones in the future.

The Legal Foundations

You can think of the legal structure as the community's invisible scaffolding—it's not what makes the place beautiful, but without it, the structure won't stand for long. The legal form determines who owns the land, how decisions are made, who is responsible for taxes, and what happens if someone leaves or passes away.

Many people who dream of community are surprised to learn that there isn't one "standard" way to organize it. It's up to each community to decide how it will be structured and each structure carries a set of trade-offs—between flexibility and formality, equity and accessibility, personal ownership and collective stewardship.

The simplest and most common starting point, at least in the US, is an **LLC** (Limited Liability Company). It's relatively easy to set up, provides liability protection, and allows members to jointly own land. It's a great starting place for a forming group still figuring things out. But LLCs are just one option.

Some communities take a longer view and choose to form a **Community Land Trust**—a nonprofit that owns the land permanently for the benefit of residents. Homeowners lease the land rather than owning it outright, which helps keep housing affordable and removes land from the speculative market. It's a beautiful model if your goal is long-term affordability, though it can take more time, money, and expertise to set up.

Cohousing neighborhoods often use an **HOA (Homeowners Association)** structure—a familiar format that banks and municipalities understand, but infused with a much friendlier, resident-run approach (not your typical HOA!). Each household owns its home, while the HOA manages the shared land and common house.

In **cooperatives**, members own shares in the collective rather than individual properties. It's a democratic model—one member, one vote—and it often attracts those who value equality and shared decision-making over private ownership. The downside is that financing can be harder to secure, since lenders are less familiar with the model.

Some groups also form **nonprofits**, especially when their mission includes education, sustainability, or social service. Nonprofits can receive tax-deductible donations and own tax-exempt land. The trade-off is that residents can't hold equity through the nonprofit itself, though some communities use a **hybrid model**, combining a nonprofit for shared assets with a cooperative or LLC for resident homes.

A **PMA** (Private Membership Association) is becoming increasingly popular among new communities because it allows groups to operate more privately and with fewer layers of government regulation. Some communities also choose to establish a new spiritual or religious identity, or they are already functioning as a spiritual group, which enables them to operate under a **nonprofit religious structure**.

Often communities end up using multiple entities. One entity holds the land; another runs the programs; a third might own shared businesses or rental housing. Just make sure you have clear written agreements between all these entities to clarify how each functions and relates to the other.

The key takeaway? **Start simple.** The legal form is the container, not the heart. Choose something that matches your stage of development, document your intentions clearly, and plan to adapt as your community grows.

Governance and Decision-Making: The Invisible Glue

If legal structure is the skeleton, governance is the nervous system—the way information moves, decisions get made, and feedback travels through the whole body.

Every community has to answer one unavoidable question: **"Who decides?"**

In most modern societies, we're used to majority voting—whoever gets the most votes wins. But in community life, decisions are often more personal and interconnected. The question isn't just what's best for me, but what's best for *us*. That shift in mindset changes everything.

I've heard it said that Geoph Kozeny, a legend in the communities movement, was once asked what the best decision-making process is. His response:

"The best process is the one the members trust."

Trust is what makes any system work. You can have the most elegant flowchart in the world, but if people don't feel heard or respected, the structure will eventually collapse.

Different communities find different paths to that trust.

Some use **consensus**, where all voices are included and the group seeks a decision that everyone can accept (or everyone minus one, depending on the model). When done well, consensus can be deeply empowering, creating decisions that reflect the wisdom of the whole. When done poorly (without solid facilitation and delegation to smaller committees), it can drag on for hours, exhausting everyone involved.

Others use **sociocracy**, a newer cousin of consensus based on *consent*. Proposals still move through rounds of discussion and attempts to address any concerns, but then, instead of asking "does everyone agree?" sociocracy asks, "are there any reasoned objections?" Proposals move forward if they're "good enough for now, safe enough to try," with built-in feedback loops and regular review. Sociocracy is also an entire governance system, ideal for larger groups that appreciate structure and can commit to learning its intricacies. The Sociocracy For All organization is an excellent resource for such learning.

Smaller groups sometimes lean on **do-ocracy**, where whoever takes initiative gets to decide, as long as it doesn't harm others or contradict community values. This works beautifully in high-trust environments where people are empowered to act, though it can cause friction if communication breaks down.

And yes—some communities have what's jokingly called a **benevolent dictatorship**, where a founder or long-term leader holds final say. As unappealing as that may sound, it can work in early phases when decisions need to be made quickly and vision needs to stay coherent. The important part is transparency: everyone knows how decisions are made, and there's a pathway for shared leadership as the group matures.

Most communities, in reality, use **hybrids**. They might use sociocracy for internal teams, consensus for deciding on new members, and voting for financial decisions. They might invent new systems or draw from diverse cultural traditions. Ways of Council, Circling, heart circles, authentic relating, meditation, tarot readings, or talking sticks may be used in combination with more formal governance systems.

For example, when I lived at Sirius Community in Massachusetts, we would quietly meditate together for 30 minutes before starting every meeting, which did seem to have a beneficial effect on the quality of our decision-making.

If you're visiting a community, listen closely when members describe how decisions are made. Do they roll their eyes or light up with pride? Do they speak of endless meetings or constructive dialogue? Their tone will tell you more about the health of their governance than any diagram ever could.

Money, Membership, and the Flow of Daily Life

Beyond structure and governance lies the part that is hardest to capture on paper: the everyday dance of cooperation.

Most intentional communities rely on some form of shared budget, with members contributing dues or work hours toward maintenance, insurance, and shared spaces. How those systems are managed, and how transparent they are, can make or break trust. A healthy community makes its finances visible, understandable, and fair.

Beyond money, the exchange of energy, labor, and non-material contributions is what keeps the heart of any community pumping.

Some groups, especially income-sharing communities, try to make as many contributions visible as possible, including forms of labor that mainstream society often takes for granted, such as childcare. These communities can track contributions in detailed systems. That is the far end of the spectrum. Most communities simply ask for a few hours of volunteer time each month, with tasks suited to each person's abilities.

During the growing season, we have work parties in my community. It is a fun way to tackle bigger projects together. We hold a very relaxed view of contributions, understanding that people go through different phases of life. Building a home, raising a family, or navigating illness all shape how much someone can give at any moment. Contributions naturally ebb and flow.

Membership processes also reveal a great deal about how a group functions. Some communities have a formal path that includes an orientation, a trial period, and a mutual feedback process before someone becomes a full member. Others are looser, letting relationships develop more organically. There is no single right way, but clarity always helps. People need to know what is expected of them and what they can expect in return.

Communities also hold us through all the cycles of life, including the profound threshold of death. When someone in the community is dying, the support can be extraordinary. People come together for caregiving, companionship, and presence. Grief is shared rather than carried alone. Many communities create grief rituals, green burials, or conscious inheritance practices that reflect their shared values. Death in community becomes not only a moment of sorrow, but also a powerful expression of connection, continuity, and love.

At the center of every community are *the relationships.*

Bylaws and meeting notes matter, but let's remember that they exist so people can focus on what is most important: living, working, and growing together.

Even in the strongest communities, daily life is not always smooth. Shared work, shared finances, and shared decisions bring people closer, but they also highlight differences in communication, expectations, and needs. These tensions are not failures. They are opportunities to understand one another more fully.

In the next chapter, we will explore how conflict shows up in community and what to do when it happens.

WHEN CONFLICT HAPPENS

> "We might define true community as that place where the person you least want to live with lives."
> —Parker Palmer

The tension in the room was heavier than the rain beating down outside. Its source sat in the middle of our circle: a thirteen-inch laptop, rotated now and then so the person on Zoom could see who was speaking. Ostensibly, the person chose to join virtually due to an illness, but we figured there was another unspoken reason. A string of heated emails had escalated to this moment. The last message had landed like a bomb. I'm leaving.

No one had ever left before. We had a process on paper, but doing it in real life was new territory. Who was owed what? How would we account for untraceable contributions? What would happen to shared dreams for the future? Was a legal battle about to unfold?

The conflict consumed our small community for half a year, and its echoes still linger. Yet the experience brought unexpected transformation. New families moved in. A fresh chapter began. Transparency deepened. Agreements were rewritten on blank paper. We made it out alive, indeed, stronger than ever.

If you have been reading along, you already know the spoiler. Real community is not tidy. People are different. Needs collide. Schedules slip. Feelings get rubbed raw. That is not a failure of community. It is simply what happens when humans live in close orbit.

The question is never "Will there be conflict?"
The question is "What will we do with it?"

Healthy communities do not avoid conflict. They name it, work with it, and grow sturdier because of it. This chapter is your field guide for navigating those moments.

I will not pretend to be a perfect communicator or the world's best facilitator. I am simply a neighbor trying to live well with other humans. What follows is what I have learned along the way.

Normalizing Conflict

Conflict in intentional communities is not just inevitable—it's essential.

Most of us grew up with scarce practice in honest, skillful disagreement. School rewarded right answers over curiosity. Families taught us to avoid hard feelings or blow past them. Then we show up to an intentional community and suddenly share kitchens, budgets, gardens, playrooms, parking, and decision-making. Of course it's triggering.

A community that claims "we never have conflict" is waving a quiet red flag. Either tough stuff gets buried, or people don't feel safe enough to bring it up. Conflict isn't the problem. Avoidance is.

As Scott Peck writes in *The Different Drum*, "Pseudocommunity is conflict-avoiding: true community is conflict-resolving."

When a big conflict erupts, like it did in my community a few years ago, it rarely appears out of nowhere. Tensions are usually simmering beneath the surface long before. A healthy conflict culture normalizes frequent micro-eruptions. People speak up early. They listen with curiosity. They release tension before it turns into resentment.

A culture of giving and receiving feedback helps immensely. When someone offers you feedback, especially when it stings, try simply saying, "Thank you for the feedback," and give yourself time to reflect. Not every piece of feedback is yours to take in, but staying open to it is how we grow.

In this way, we keep the pot gently simmering rather than letting it boil over.

Know Your Default Moves

Honestly, group conflict still terrifies me. I would rather hide in my house for days than cross paths with someone I am struggling with. Because I know this about myself, I try to gently push toward the fear instead of away from it.

You may be different. You might be a fiery spirit who charges into conflict ready to hash things out. Or you might be a peacemaker who lets that fiery person steamroll all over you.

We each bring a style to tense moments. One classic map, Thomas-Kilmann Conflict Mode Instrument (TKI), names five:

- **Avoiding** – step back, delay, go quiet
- **Accommodating** – keep the peace, give in
- **Competing** – push hard for a result
- **Compromising** – split the difference
- **Collaborating** – slow down to find a win-win

None are "bad." Each helps in certain conditions. Trouble comes when one style runs the whole show. Add personality patterns (Enneagram,

Myers-Briggs Type Indicator [MBTI]), family norms, culture, even the room's color and noise level, and you can see why two people might read the same moment very differently.

Tools for Navigating Conflict

Self-Awareness

The most reliable tool for navigating community conflict is your own self-awareness. Notice your triggers, patterns, and habitual reactions. Do you tend to withdraw? Get defensive? Try to fix others? Seek approval? Becoming aware of these tendencies gives you choice.

Practices that support self-awareness include journaling, mindfulness, somatic work, therapy, or asking trusted friends for honest reflection. Most of us were never taught these skills in school, yet they form the backbone of healthy community life.

Nonviolent Communication

Nonviolent Communication or NVC (sometimes called compassionate communication), developed by Marshall Rosenberg, offers a framework built on needs-awareness, empathy, and non-judgmental expression. Many communities use NVC trainings to build shared language around emotional literacy.

However, like any tool, NVC can be misused. When wielded rigidly or without emotional fluency, it can feel performative or even manipulative. Some communities grow cautious of it for this reason. The key is authenticity, not reciting a script.

Used skillfully, NVC can help people soften, listen more deeply, and stay connected during difficult conversations.

Other Helpful Modalities

NVC is far from the only tool available. Communities around the world experiment with—and often blend—multiple frameworks, such as:

- **The Ways of Council**, a circle-based practice for deep listening and honest speaking
- **Restorative Circles**, which focus on repairing relationships rather than assigning blame
- **Authentic Relating and Circling**, which build presence and emotional awareness
- **Imago Dialogue**, a structured technique for reflective speaking and hearing
- **Possibility Management**, centered on emotional responsibility and conscious communication
- **Integral Family Systems,** to understand your different inner "parts" and how they fit together into a more balanced whole

Each community adopts practices that fit its culture.

One famous federation of communities in Italy, Damanhur, even stages mock battles with foam swords and shields as a playful way to release tension before it becomes toxic.

The tool matters less than the shared commitment to honesty, respect, and accountability.

Anticipating Conflict: The Five Ps

Thriving communities tend to be proactive rather than reactive. In cohousing circles, it is often said that most community conflicts boil down to "The Three Ps":

- **Pets**
- **Parenting**
- **Parking**

To which many communities add two more:

- **Participation**
- **Pennies (Money)**

And there are even more P's worth pondering! For a piece that's both practical and playful, peek at Laird Schaub's piece "Minding the 'P's for Cues" in *Communities* magazine (in the Summer 2009 issue), in which much of the text is written in words starting with—yes—**P**.

If you'd like to pursue Laird's writing more deeply, his blog at **communityandconsensus.blogspot.com** is a treasure trove of community wisdom from one of the key figures behind the formation of the FIC and the shaping of the intentional communities movement in North America.

Group Agreements

Shared agreements act as the immune system of a community. They do not eliminate conflict, but they keep it from turning into interpersonal wildfire. Agreements often cover:

- Communication norms
- The group's decision-making model

- Expectations for chores, meetings, and shared responsibilities
- Policies around pets, children, guests, and finances
- Boundaries around personal space and noise

The most effective agreements are co-created and regularly revisited. They evolve as the group evolves. Beware the member who waves a group agreement in the air like a battle flag. Agreements are meant to help resolve conflicts, not create new ones.

A Simple Conflict Resolution Framework

Every intentional community benefits from having a clear, step-by-step conflict process. Below is a simple pattern I've seen widely used by communities:

Step 1: Direct Conversation

Most conflicts can be resolved through a direct, honest conversation. Yet many people find this step the hardest. They would rather talk to anyone else about the issue first. This "triangling" or back-channeling can quietly erode trust.

If someone comes to you with a complaint about another person, gently redirect them. Encourage them to speak directly to the person involved and avoid sharing something they would not want repeated.

Direct conversation can resolve nearly all conflicts when it happens early. If for some reason it feels more safe, each party can invite a witness or support person to be present for the conversation.

Step 2: Mediation

If direct conversation is not enough, involve a neutral mediator. This might be someone from a designated care or conflict team with the community, or an outside facilitator who brings neutrality and structure. Each party may want a witness or support person present, in addition to the mediator.

Mediation is a valuable skill for anyone involved in intentional community. Those who learn it often find it useful both within their communities and beyond them. If you would like to learn more, or to hire a mediator to support your group, one strong recommendation is the classes and services offered by Karen Gimnig, co-author, along with Yana Ludwig, of *The Cooperative Culture Handbook*.

Step 3: Wider Group Involvement

If mediation fails or the issue affects more people, it could come to a conflict team or small group. Especially in larger communities, conflicts tend to go through small-group work before being brought to the whole community. In smaller communities, news travels fast, and the whole community may be involved earlier on. Every attempt is made to hear all perspectives, often through a formal circle or forum, before any collective decisions are made.

Some options for wider group social processes that support conflict resolution and deeper understanding include: Restorative Circles, ZEGG Forum, and Council Practice.

Step 4: Asking Someone to Leave (Rare)

This is always a last resort. Asking someone to leave their home is profound and, in many places, legally complex. Communities should have clear policies that include due process and safeguards against unfairness.

Of course, the linchpin of a healthy conflict resolution process is a healthy membership process. Often the best remedy for conflict is screening for emotional maturity and culture fit long before someone moves in. Once they are a member, though, every effort should be made to work through challenges together before considering a parting of ways.

Understanding the Natural Stages of Group Development

Psychologist Bruce Tuckman's Forming, Storming, Norming, Performing model gives a helpful lens for understanding why conflict arises.

- **Forming**: Polite, cautious, honeymoon energy
- **Storming**: Differences emerge; tension becomes visible
- **Norming**: The group develops shared norms and expectations
- **Performing**: Cooperation becomes fluid and effective

Communities cycle through these stages repeatedly. Every new member, crisis, or major decision invites another round of forming and storming before the group stabilizes again.

I see this pattern play out even during our week-long Ecovillage Tours. At the beginning, everyone is kind and courteous. By day three or four, little frictions emerge—someone's always late, another person talks too much, or there's disagreement about how we spend group time. But towards the end, something shifts. People begin to speak more honestly, give each other grace, and work together to improve the group dynamic. We often leave having achieved genuine camaraderie.

Our Best Teacher

Earlier in this book, I described community as a hall of mirrors. The people around you reflect your strengths, your blind spots, and the habits you did not know you had. Another helpful image is the rock tumbler. You put in a handful of rough stones, they knock around together, and over time they come out smoother and more polished.

Community works the same way. We bump into each other. Our edges get tested. With patience and honesty, those edges soften.

Conflict does not mean a community is failing. It means people are being real with each other. With shared tools, clear agreements, and a willingness to stay present, conflict becomes one of the best teachers we have.

PART VII:

CLOSING THOUGHTS

A WINTER DAY IN COMMUNITY

"We need four hugs a day for survival, eight for maintenance, and twelve for growth."
—Virginia Satir

Today it snowed all day, as it does here in northern Vermont.

I spent most of the morning indoors with the woodstove blazing and my cat curled up, sleeping away while I moved from meeting to meeting. Thursdays are my "chore day," so I venture out to mind the chickens between calls.

Winter is easy because you just need to water, feed, and collect the scant eggs our ladies produce this time of year. In the non-freezing seasons it's a different story: watering the beds in our big hoop house (acquired thanks to an ag grant), tending to urgent needs in the outside garden, and collecting *way* more eggs than our community can possibly eat (the extras get sold or gifted away).

It can be much to do, but I only need to be on for one day a week, trusting my neighbors to care for things on their days and covering for each other when we travel.

Around dusk the snowfall let up, so I headed out again to light the woodstove in our Earthship greenhouse to keep the plants from freezing overnight. I harvested some arugula for dinner while I was at it.

Then my neighbor came by to fill a bucket of water for our sauna later that evening. We caught up about our recent Thanksgivings. Then another neighbor appeared, dropping off food for the community freezer. We hugged hello and chatted about summer plans—my upcoming wedding, a big camping trip we want to do together, and when we should meet next to order seeds for the garden.

Now is the time to make summer plans, to help carry us through the cold months still ahead.

By then the snow had really piled up and the kids decided it was time for fun. The little ones had gone sledding during the day. But the "big kids," having outgrown the thrill of sledding, decided to level up the antics: biking down the steepest snowy hill with headlamps in the dark, falling into fluffy drifts with pure glee.

Around this time I got ready to sauna, something a few of us neighborhood women do about once a week. I love the long, deep chats we have by candlelight. I love listening—taking mental notes about everything they share regarding childbirth and motherhood. So much of our conversation centers around the daughters they are raising and the relationships we all have with our own mothers. I feel grateful beyond measure to be learning from them, quietly preparing myself to raise my own kids someday in this sweet community I get to call home.

As soon as I'm warmed to the bones, I place my towel on the snow and lay out to face the stars.

The land is so still now, asleep. Gazing at the galaxy transports me to a place beyond the daily concerns—finishing this book, finishing the house, answering an overflowing inbox, tracking never-ending to-dos.

The heat from my body sinks me deeper into the soft blanket of this land. My sense of connection expands to include the larger surface I lie upon, this globe spinning and speeding through a vast universe.

We are here for but a moment. Why not embrace every chance for connection?

DEFENDING YOUR CHOICE

> "Forget conventionalisms; forget what the world thinks of you stepping out of your place; think your best thoughts, speak your best words, work your best works."
>
> —Susan B. Anthony

When you first tell people you want to live in an intentional community, prepare for a few raised eyebrows.

"So…you want to join a commune?"
"Do those even still exist?"
"Will you be allowed to leave?"
"What if we never see you again?"

Yes, all questions I've been asked by some of my closest family members.

The jokes and skepticism often come first, followed by nervous proddings about privacy, money, and "what happens if it doesn't work out." If you're partnered, you might also encounter a quieter version of the same doubts from the person you love most.

None of this means you're on the wrong path. It simply means you're stepping into territory most people don't yet understand.

You're Not the Crazy One

Let's start here: **you are not crazy for wanting to live in community.**

What's strange is how we live now.

For nearly all of human history, people lived in small, interdependent groups—villages, tribes, extended families. We evolved to share resources, stories, and care. Only in the past century have we shifted to a culture of isolated households and high mobility, where it's possible to spend years in one neighborhood without learning the names of those next door.

Loneliness has become so widespread that the former US Surgeon General declared it a public health crisis. Research from Brigham Young University found that social isolation increases the risk of premature death by nearly 30%—a statistic rivaling the effects of smoking or obesity.

So no, you're not crazy for craving something more connected. You're responding, quite sanely, to an unhealthy system. Intentional communities are not a fringe experiment; they're a return to what has always made us human.

How to Talk About It

When explaining your interest to friends and family, your tone matters more than your talking points. People who care about you may simply be worried—about your safety, your finances, or whether you'll still come home for the holidays. Respond with warmth and curiosity. Let them ask. And whenever possible, translate "community living" into language they already understand.

You might say:

"It's like an old-fashioned neighborhood, where people actually know each other."

"It's a planned residential community that shares gardens and amenities."
"Think of it as collaborative housing—private homes with shared spaces."
"We're interested in sustainable, community-oriented living."

Those phrases feel familiar and approachable. They evoke small-town nostalgia rather than 1960s communes. Words like *collective* or *commune* can sound intimidating, even if technically accurate. Meet people where they are.

A friend of mine once told his parents he was moving into "a co-op," and they immediately imagined a dormitory filled with unwashed dishes. When he switched to "a neighborhood that runs its own gardens and common house," the conversation softened. The difference was only language, but language builds bridges.

Reframing the Fears

It helps to anticipate the big worries and answer them simply.

Privacy: Yes, people have their own homes or rooms. Doors close. There's plenty of personal space.

Finances: Communities use normal structures—rental, ownership, or co-ownership—and often employ lawyers and accountants like anywhere else.

Freedom: Membership is voluntary. You can leave anytime. Communities have clear exit procedures in writing.

Diversity: Not every community is rural, countercultural, or "hippie." Many are suburban, urban, professional, intergenerational, and even quite ordinary, just friendlier.

Sharing credible resources also reassures people that this isn't just your personal whim.

Mention the *Harvard Study of Adult Development*, which found that strong relationships are the single biggest predictor of long-term happiness and health. Or the *Blue Zones* research, which shows that the longest-living populations on Earth all have one thing in common: close-knit social networks. According to the Centers for Disease Control and Prevention (CDC), social isolation raises mortality risk nearly as much as smoking fifteen cigarettes a day. Those statistics make an excellent case that community living isn't fringe, it's preventive medicine.

When friends or family question your choice, remind them that this isn't about giving up individuality. It's about rebuilding connection.

Showing, Not Telling

Sometimes no amount of explanation will suffice until people see it with their own eyes.

Photos of smiling neighbors around a shared meal or children running between homes communicate more than an hour of talking. You might share recent media coverage—articles in *The New York Times* and *The Conversation* describing the "new generation of self-created villages," or a TEDx talk like Bianca Heyming's *Intentional Communities: 50% Less Hippie Than You'd Expect*. These stories help normalize what you're exploring.

Better yet, invite your family to visit someday. Most people who step foot in a well-functioning community are surprised by how ordinary it feels. The smell of soup from a common kitchen and the laughter of neighbors repairing a garden gate will do the work for you.

Until then, find your own support circle—people who *do* understand this calling. Surround yourself with allies who remind you that you're not alone in wanting a more cooperative life.

When You Love Someone Who's Not Yet Onboard

If you're in a partnership where one of you is eager and the other is hesitant, take heart. This tension is common, and workable.

Living in community together can be one of the most rewarding adventures a couple can take, but only if both partners walk in *willingly*.

I've seen it too many times: one person dives into research, joins forums, and schedules tours while the other hangs back, praying this is just a phase. It rarely ends well when one half drags the other along. The goal is alignment, not persuasion.

Start with conversation, not logistics. Ask each other what you truly want from your next chapter of life. What does "home" mean to you? What do you crave more of—quiet, social connection, nature, security, freedom? Where do you feel most alive?

As you talk, listen for overlap. Even if your partner insists they're "not a community person," they probably still value belonging, beauty, and a sense of safety. You're just using different words to describe the same need.

Exercises for Couples

Compare Your Visions

One simple way to start aligning is by completing the **Community Wishlist Worksheet** separately. Each of you lists ideal features—location, size, amenities, values, housing style—and then you compare notes. Seeing your priorities side by side often reveals both shared goals and easy compromises.

Take the Quiz Together

If you want a playful entry point, try the **Community Type Quiz** on my website at **communityfinders.com/quiz**. It takes two minutes and can spark hours of conversation about what each of you imagines. Some couples discover they're far more aligned than they expected.

Try a "Community Vacation"

Book a short stay at an ecovillage, cohousing community, or retreat center. Approach it like a weekend getaway, not a sales pitch. Visit the gardens, share one meal, and observe how people interact. Afterwards, debrief honestly: what felt exciting, what felt uncomfortable, and what would need to change for it to work long-term? Many reluctant partners soften after they experience real-world examples that look nothing like their fears.

Learn Together

Watch a few short videos or read books about community living. Robert Waldinger's TED talk *What Makes a Good Life?* offers science; *The Art of Community* by Charles Vogl offers heart. Learning side by side builds a common language.

Commit to a Shared Process

If you decide to keep exploring, agree on ground rules. Perhaps you'll visit two communities within the next six months, spend no more than a set budget, and decide afterward whether to continue. Clear agreements make the journey collaborative instead of coercive.

When Loved Ones Stay Skeptical

Not everyone will understand, and that's okay. Some people may always view your choice as strange or idealistic. You don't have to win them over. Let your life speak for itself. Over time, as they see you thriving—less stressed, more grounded—they'll begin to trust your path.

Invite them to visit once you're settled. Let them experience the joy of kids playing safely in shared courtyards, the ease of neighbors lending tools, the laughter at potlucks under string lights. These quiet, ordinary moments are the best ambassadors for communal life.

And if they still don't come around, remember: the strength of your conviction doesn't depend on others' approval. Every pioneer faces skepticism at first.

And perhaps someday, when you've found your place and your people, those same skeptical voices might call and say, "You know that community thing you were talking about? Tell me more."

THE FUTURE OF COMMUNITY

> "The future is already here. It's just not evenly distributed."
>
> —William Gibson

If there's one thing I hope this book has made clear, it's that intentional community is not a fringe idea. It is part of a profound cultural shift already underway.

Across the world, people are reimagining how they live together. From urban cohousing in London, to ecovillages in Costa Rica, to cooperative apartments in Los Angeles, the modern movement toward community living is growing faster than most people realize. What began as radical experiments in shared living has become, for many, a practical and hopeful response to some of the defining challenges of our time.

And yet, we still have a ways to go. Community living is not yet so common that it feels unremarkable, or so expected that living alone would seem unusual. We are still in a moment where choosing community often requires intention, explanation, and courage.

In this final section, let's explore the challenges that remain, the opportunities ahead, and where our growing movement toward intentional community may be headed next.

Overlapping Crises

We live in a paradoxical time—hyperconnected yet deeply isolated. Rates of loneliness have skyrocketed across all demographics.

Meanwhile, housing costs have reached crisis levels. Millions are priced out of homeownership or even stable rent. In some regions, entire generations face permanent displacement.

Environmental pressures are escalating as well. Deforestation, the corporatization of agriculture, fragile food systems, natural disasters, and water scarcity are increasingly intertwined. Together, they are displacing people and communities across the globe.

Intentional communities offer tangible responses to these problems. By sharing resources, they make housing more affordable. By restoring neighborly interdependence, they ease the ache of isolation. By caring for place, they foster resiliency and regeneration.

In mainstream housing, you pick a house and hope the neighbors are decent. In an intentional community, the model is flipped. What if everyone had the chance to meet the neighbors first and only then decide whether to make a home among them?

This isn't idealism. It's practical compassion. It's acknowledging that the way we've been living doesn't work for everyone, and the solutions might come not from institutions, but from one another.

But for the solutions that intentional communities demonstrate to catch on, people need to know about them to begin with. Therein lies the role of research.

A Call for Research

I'm often asked seemingly simple questions: How many intentional communities are there? How many new ones are starting? Is the number growing?

I do my best to answer based on the information available, the trends I see, and what colleagues in this space report. Still, I wish I could point to solid, comprehensive data.

One of the biggest hurdles to understanding the rise of intentional communities is that no single organization tracks them fully. Many communities are small, informal, or constantly evolving. Some identify as ecovillages or cohousing projects. Others call themselves cooperatives, land trusts, or regenerative living networks. Countless more do not use any label at all.

As a result, accurate data is difficult to obtain. Directories like the one hosted by the FIC list over 1,200 active communities worldwide, yet we know this represents only a fraction of what exists. Many groups never register publicly, and some quietly thrive below the radar for decades.

There is an urgent need for better research. Sociological, economic, environmental, and cultural studies are all needed to understand the real impacts of community living. We need universities to examine how intentional communities affect mental health, social cohesion, environmental footprints, affordability, and overall well-being. We need evidence that can inform zoning decisions, housing policy, and urban planning.

So to the researchers, students, and policymakers reading this: please, study this movement.

For those inclined toward research, organizations such as the International Communal Studies Association and the US-focused Communal Studies Association welcome new members.

Intentional communities are part of the solution to the crises of our time. We need the data to prove it.

Community in the Mainstream

Even if the data isn't fully there yet, public perception *is* shifting.

Major media outlets such as *The New York Times*, *The Guardian*, the BBC, and *The Washington Post* now publish coverage of intentional communities that is surprisingly positive. Articles highlight cohousing as a model for aging in place, regenerative villages as part of climate solutions, and cooperative housing as a lifeline for young families.

YouTube videos and documentaries are beginning to explore communal living as a viable, contemporary lifestyle rather than a 1960s throwback. On social media, hashtags like #cohousing and #ecovillage attract millions of views, signaling growing curiosity and engagement.

I've been part of several conversations with producers in the early stages of developing an intentional community television series designed for a broad audience. These projects are slow to move forward, but the interest itself is telling. It feels less like a question of *if* and more like *when* intentional community becomes the focus of a mainstream series.

Something has shifted. Community living is no longer just a curiosity. It is becoming a real, visible option.

The Question of Access

And yet, not everyone has that option.

Many intentional communities remain accessible primarily to those with time, education, and financial resources. Land is expensive. Zoning laws are outdated. Legal and financial systems often work *against* collective ownership.

Meanwhile, the people who could most benefit from stable, cooperative housing—low-income families, single parents, essential workers, elders on fixed incomes—face the steepest barriers to entry.

If intentional communities are to become a true movement for societal transformation, they must become accessible to everyone.

That means supporting affordable housing cooperatives, inclusive land trusts, and creative financing models. It means advocating for zoning reform that allows small-scale shared-living, and multi-family arrangements. It means inviting in diversity—across race, age, ability, and income—and learning from the many cultures that have practiced collective living for centuries.

The future of this movement depends on widening the circle, not closing it.

I'm hopeful we will get there. Already the accessibility of community living has risen tremendously in recent years, due in no small part to how the Covid era forever changed the way people think about home and work.

Remote work untethered millions from the office, freeing them to choose where and how they live. For many, that freedom sparked a simple question: *If I can live anywhere, why not somewhere meaningful? Why not among people I actually know?*

And while some forms of community still feel impossibly expensive to join, a growing range of co-buying, retrofit, modular home, tiny home, and subsidized housing communities are making this lifestyle attainable in creative ways.

But now, as we widen the circle of who can belong, we must also reckon with the tools that will shape the future of belonging itself.

The AI Revolution

AI (Artificial Intelligence) and especially AGI (Artificial General Intelligence) are reshaping civilization in ways we are only beginning to understand.

For a while, I thought Covid would be the defining historical shift of my lifetime. But the rapid acceleration of AI—and the technologies created in its wake—is becoming the Industrial Revolution of our era.

Like the original Industrial Revolution, this one brings upheaval. People will be displaced. Livelihoods lost. Entire industries transformed. And nature, once again, is paying the price as massive energy demands fuel new technologies.

As with any technology, the values we embed into AI determine its impact. Will it be developed for the good of all, or the profit of a few? How will our highest human values be protected? Just when the AI revolution calls for unprecedented global coordination, we seem to be slipping deeper into the silos of competitive nation-states.

And yet, AI may not spell doom.

Already we've seen breakthroughs that would have been impossible without it. The application of AI to the protein-folding problem, one of the main unsolved problems in molecular biology—and critically important, the open sharing of those discoveries—has sparked advances in biology and medicine that verge on miraculous. AI is also being used to dramatically improve early warning systems for floods, wildfires, and extreme heat, helping communities prepare before disasters strike.

Thankfully, organizations like the Cooperative AI Foundation are now supporting research to ensure that advanced intelligence learns cooperation, not domination. While intentional communities cannot control the accelerating pace of AI development or the directions it will take, we can choose how we respond. Modeling cooperative values has never mattered more.

Tech Pulls Us Apart and Can Bring Together

What does modeling cooperation look like in a technological age?

Technology too often separates us. As Sherry Turkle writes, we are increasingly "alone together." We're physically near but mentally absorbed in our screens.

Yet those very screens can also be tools of connection, creativity, and collaboration when used with intention. Across the globe, communities are experimenting with tools that were unimaginable a decade ago.

The rise of DAOs (Decentralized Autonomous Organizations), like Traditional Dream Factory in Portugal, shows how blockchain can help groups manage shared resources, track contributions, and create transparent agreements. The Monastic Academy, a contemplative community not far from where I live in Vermont, is experimenting directly with the question: *How do we ensure that intelligence is guided by wisdom and compassion as it scales?*

Even my own community, which is fairly low-tech (especially where the kids are concerned), has begun experimenting with AI to help streamline our bylaws and clarify our governance documents.

The recent articles in *Communities* (in the Winter 2025 issue) are a great read for anyone wanting to learn more about the impacts of AI and modern technology within the communities movement.

Not a Return to the Past

Community living is not about going backward.

Some communities do feel like a step into an earlier era—horse-drawn plows in the fields, people living simply from the land, traditional crafts brought back to life. It is easy to romanticize the past. I fall into that nostalgia sometimes too. But we also know the past held its own share of hardship. Alongside the beauty were violence, exploitation, and profound suffering.

Intentional community is not an attempt to resurrect some lost golden age. It is about weaving together the best of the past with the best of the present to create a resilient future.

Technology is part of that present. And it is almost certainly here to stay.

I love watching back-to-the-land farmers document their homesteading journeys on YouTube. I love seeing start-up communities use digital tools to organize themselves more effectively. I love the visionary artists and futurists imagining worlds where technology becomes a partner rather than a threat. And I love seeing intentional-community networks collaborate with new tools to build directories, matchmaking platforms, and online forums that make it easier than ever for people to find the right community.

Tech will continue to shape how we gather. But instead of replacing community, it may become one of the things that makes community more possible.

My Hope for the Future

During interviews, I'm often asked how I stay hopeful about the future. I always give the same answer, and I hope it does not sound like a cop-out, because it is genuinely how I feel.

My hope is not based in the future.

The truth is, I have no idea what is going to happen, *especially in the long term*. Will AI turn on us? Will ecosystem collapse render the planet uninhabitable? Will nuclear war finish the job? Will corporations and consumption drain the last of our living world? Will the aliens running things finally decide to reveal themselves?

Or will something entirely different happen? Maybe as populations stabilize, we rediscover low-consumption, land-based living supported by helpful technology. Maybe we move away from political boundaries and organize ourselves into a bioregional tapestry, or even "network states," as Balaji Srinivasan envisions. Maybe gardens take back our cities, governments choose peace, and intentional communities flourish as a new foundation for human civilization.

I can fantasize about a positive future one day, and doom-scroll the next. None of it changes how I choose to live *now*.

The hope that sustains me is rooted in the present, not in predictions.

I grow as much of my food as I can because it feels deliciously good. I love my bare feet in the dirt all summer. I love the shelves of vegetables in the cold room all winter. I love living in community—not because I think it will save humanity, but because it brings joy and meaning into my daily life. I love seeing the kids here grow up strong and free. I love the companionship, the playfulness, the shared meals, the silly moments, the sense of belonging.

I am not writing this book because I believe it will topple corporations or transform the world order (though that'd be a delightful outcome). I wrote it because it is the only book I can write. I live the life I live because it is the only life I can live.

That is where my hope comes from. Not from what might happen someday, but from choosing a way of life that brings me alive *now*.

Returning to Belonging

If you've made it to the end of this book, you already know something important about yourself: you are someone who believes a different way of living is possible.

Perhaps you have felt the tug of longing—for deeper connection, for shared purpose, for a home where your gifts matter and your presence is felt. Perhaps you've sensed that our culture's default settings are no longer enough, that we need not only new structures, but new stories for how to live well with one another.

The truth is, community is not a destination. It is a practice. A way of relating. A way of remembering that we were never meant to do life alone.

And you do not need to have it all figured out before you begin. You do not need to know which community is "the one," or whether you will join, start, or simply support one from the edges. What matters is that you follow the small signals of aliveness. Follow those things that make you feel more yourself, more connected, more human. A garden bed. A shared meal. A conversation that opens your heart. A vision that won't leave you alone.

Community begins in these tiny gestures long before it becomes land or bylaws or shared kitchens. It begins in the simple decision to show up for yourself, and then for one another.

I cannot promise you that the path will be easy. Community will stretch you, soften you, challenge you, and sometimes break your heart. But if you stay with it—if you lean into the mirrors and the rock tumbler, into the messiness and the grace—you may find yourself becoming someone more spacious, more grounded, and more alive.

And perhaps, one day, you will look around and realize that you are living inside the very future you once longed for.

Not because the world suddenly changed, but because *you* did. Because you made choices rooted in connection rather than fear. Because you planted yourself somewhere and said, "Let's try building something beautiful together."

This book is not an instruction manual. It is an invitation. A companion. A reminder that community is not only possible—it is already happening, quietly and boldly, in backyards and forests and cities across the world.

The next step belongs to you.

WHERE TO GO NEXT

You may notice that this book does not end with a long printed bibliography or pages of resource lists. That was a deliberate choice.

The world of intentional communities is constantly evolving—organizations change names, websites shift, new projects emerge, and trainings come and go. A static list would become outdated almost the moment this book goes to print. Instead of offering you a snapshot that may fade, I wanted to create a resource that can grow and stay current.

That's why I've built an online companion page for this book: **communityfinders.com/book1**

There, you'll find:

- An up-to-date bibliography with links to books, organizations, and research mentioned throughout these chapters
- Worksheets and tools, including the Community Wishlist and Community Resume
- Videos, interviews, and additional learning for wherever you are on your community journey
- New resources as they emerge in the movement

This book ends here, but your journey doesn't. Everything you need to keep going is waiting for you online.

If QR codes are your thing, I have one for you here to easily scan and get to **communityfinders.com/book1**

AUTHOR NOTES AND ACKNOWLEDGMENTS

Intentional community is not one thing. It is many things to many different people, and its meaning continually shifts across cultures, history, and everyday life. My challenge has been to honor that breadth while still making the idea accessible to newcomers.

When choosing the cover for this book, I shared a handful of top designs on social media and invited friends, clients, colleagues, and total strangers to weigh in. The responses were wonderfully varied. Many people loved the teacups and imagined diverse neighbors gathering around them. When I first saw the design, I thought, wow, those cups could easily be sitting on the coffee table during one of our community meetings. It's not really about the cups themselves, but about the conversation, connection, and nourishment they represent.

Some people didn't like that design—or any of the designs I shared. That's okay too. Community touches something deep within us that is incredibly hard to capture in a 6×9-inch book cover, or even in several hundred pages of text. Trying to do justice to the magic, the mystery, and the mundane of community is a lifelong task.

Still, I want to say thank you to everyone who offered feedback in big and small ways, helping shape what this book has become, including the gaps and the places where I inevitably came up short.

As nebulous as intentional community can be, it is not untrodden ground. I'm a relative newbie to the modern movement—one that has been strengthening for decades. This book rests on the work, wisdom, and persistence of many who came before me, and I offer gratitude to those who have tended this movement with such care.

Chris Roth graciously agreed to edit this book, and I am immensely grateful not only for his technical editing but also for the depth of knowledge he brings from his years as editor of *Communities* magazine. It has been reassuring to have his eyes on this text, helping keep me grounded in, and connected to, the canon of community writing that has come before. I'm blessed to have learned directly from many of the authors who shaped that canon.

I carry lasting impressions from my early twenties, spent in countless board meetings for the Global Ecovillage Network and the Foundation for Intentional Community. Both online gatherings and in-person meetings in communities around the world were formative. I witnessed the beauty and the struggle of our attempts to create truly cooperative organizations within a wider culture that is, at best, re-learning cooperation and, at worst, actively resisting it.

These organizations, alongside so many others, are beacons of hope. And I'm excited for what's emerging as they deepen their collaboration. Just as nation-states unravel into divisiveness, our brave intentional community networks are tightening their weave.

To all the members of FIC, GEN, NextGEN, ICSA, and CohoUS I've had the joy of learning from and collaborating with over the years: your work, vision, and courage have shaped my understanding of what community can be. This book rests on your shoulders.

I'm especially appreciative of Nara Petrovič for being a companion through so many visits to communities. Our epic road trips across Europe helped me connect to the broader movement in ways that might never have been possible for this American otherwise. And thank you, Nara, for helping me land in the community I now call home.

To all the neighbors here in our little corner of the world—thank you, thank you, thank you. You've cheered on my audacious house-building projects, helped me settle into a new nest, and taught me that community is not just about the big gatherings (as fun as our parties are), but about the tiny daily acts of kindness and care.

Thank you as well to all of my community matchmaking clients. The hundreds of hours spent in conversation with you have quietly woven themselves into the pages of this book. Thank you for opening your stories to me and for your trust.

I am also grateful for the trust of our Ecovillage Tour participants, who come on our journeys with such curiosity to learn about community living. And to the communities who welcome our travelers—thank you for opening your doors, hearts, and busy schedules. To the team at Ecovillage Tours: thank you for helping keep everything running smoothly. I'm sure you'll all be happy to have me a bit more available once this book is finally done! (Or at least slightly more available.)

To all the founders and residents of established and newly forming intentional communities—many of whom I've had the joy of visiting or interviewing through our Virtual Tour of Intentional Community series—you are the reason this book exists at all. May your work continue to flourish.

I want to thank my family. Their constant love and support have been the stable foundation upon which I've built my life. That foundation is a privilege I'm deeply grateful for. It has also challenged me to stay connected to my roots while branching out into new perspectives. You help me stay in integrity.

Thank you to my fiancé, Nathan Oxenfeld. His work in natural vision improvement is helping me see better (literally) and see how relaxation, imagination, and playfulness are connected to well-being. I am thrilled that we are making a nest together here in a woodland of nests.

And to the woods themselves—to all the lands I've been able to roam, near and far—thank you. Thank you for giving me space to let my imagination wander and my horizons expand. And to the land right here at home: thank you for your sustenance and your calming presence.

ABOUT THE AUTHOR

Cynthia Tina helps people discover intentional community living as a path toward better housing, health, and happiness. She has visited more than 200 intentional communities around the world and lives in a Vermont ecovillage, where she resides in her self-built natural home.

This book draws on over a decade of firsthand experience to offer a practical guide to finding, joining, and thriving in community.

Her speaking, teaching, and consulting work has supported the growth of numerous community-led housing projects. Cynthia is the founder of Community Finders, which offers programs to help people join and start intentional communities, and the founder of Ecovillage Tours, which brings people on immersive journeys to regenerative communities worldwide.

Cynthia has served as a partner and educator with the Foundation for Intentional Community and is currently a trustee of the International Communal Studies Association. She previously served on the board of the Global Ecovillage Network. She holds a degree in Sustainability from Goddard College, along with certificates in Permaculture Design, Ecovillage Design, and Yoga Teacher Training.

www.ingramcontent.com/pod-product-compliance
Lightning Source LLC
Chambersburg PA
CBHW052127030426
42337CB00028B/5057